Wearable Gadgets and Technology for Meditation

By Joy Bose and Siva Prasad Bose

Published by Joy Bose

Copyright © 2024 Joy Bose

All rights reserved. No part of this book may be reproduced, or stored in a retrieval system, or transmitted in any form or by any means, electronic, mechanical, photocopying, recording, or otherwise, without express written permission of the publisher.

Contents

Dedication

This book is dedicated to all those who are practicing or have practiced mindfulness meditation.

Preface

Meditation is as old as humanity itself. It requires no more than a quiet space, a moment of stillness, and an intention to look inward. Its benefits—such as stress relief, emotional clarity, improved focus, and a deeper sense of well-being—are timeless. Some traditions even speak of meditation as a path to insight into the very nature of reality.

Yet we live in an era defined by technology. Our lives are surrounded by screens, notifications, and constant connectivity. While some may argue that modern technology distracts us from stillness, it can also serve, when used wisely, as a support for mindfulness and inner exploration.

This book is about that intersection: where ancient inner practices meet modern digital tools. Here, we explore a wide range of meditation gadgets, wearables, apps, and smart systems—from heart rate monitors and EEG headbands to smart rings, AI-guided meditation assistants, and even floatation tanks. We also include newer tools such as productivity apps, ambient smart home setups, and mindfulness-focused browser extensions.

Throughout the chapters, we share our experiences with these technologies, along with practical tips and reflections on their use. We also include cautionary advice—reminding ourselves that no gadget can replace the intention and attention that true mindfulness requires.

Whether you are a beginner trying to build a meditation habit, a tech enthusiast curious about biofeedback, or an experienced meditator looking to explore new frontiers, we hope this book serves as a guide to using technology not as a crutch, but as a companion.

May these tools help you find calm amid chaos, presence in the digital age, and support on your path toward greater clarity and peace

Chapter 1: Introduction to technology and mindfulness meditation

In this chapter, we discuss some issues related to mindfulness meditation and technology usage, and mention various ways in which to leverage technology to help with mindfulness, particularly in the area of stress reduction.

For many of us, our lives revolves around technology. For those who work full time in tech as software engineers or have online work that needs computers, technology is essential to their work in various ways. It could be sitting in front of a computer for hours on end or being glued to our mobile phones or TVs when off work. This can, however, affect us in some not so good ways. Perhaps the problems are even worse now, considering the widespread use of work from home or hybrid work due to the recent Covid pandemic.

In this chapter, we discuss a few ways in which technology can help us to cultivate mindfulness and meditation and thus become relaxed and free from stress.

1.1 Problems due to prolonged use of technology

Prolonged use of technology can lead to various problems. Some of the problems are as follows:

◇ **Physical health issues**: If we are not mindful of our posture and movement, prolonged usage of tech could lead to physical health issues. Examples are carpal tunnel syndrome (due to a bad positioning of hands when typing on a computer), back pain, neck pain, poor eyesight, lack of sleep, etc. Also in the list are issues related to poor diet and lack of exercise as a secondary result of sitting without moving in front of a computer or using a mobile for a long time.

◇ **Mental health issues**: This can include social anxiety due to widespread usage of social networking or related sites. Other related issues can be loneliness, irritability, etc. Also, too much tech usage might lead to increased stress and depression etc.

◇ **Tech addiction**: This can result when we get addicted to tech to the extent that we forget about everything else. This might be a bigger problem in younger people and teenagers. Examples are people spending hours or days playing computer games.

1.2 What is stress

Stress has many definitions. One of the early definitions are as follows:

Stress is the non-specific response of the body to any demand.

Another, more detailed definition is as follows:

Stress is the subjective state of sensing potentially adverse changes in the environment that will lead to a response that enables the animal to adapt to the changing environment.

This demand that causes stress, i.e. the adverse changes in the environment, may be caused by stressful life events or stressors, such as an upcoming exam, a job interview, getting stuck in traffic, a financial crisis, a personal life crisis and so on. The stressors can be either external events (such as death of a family member or a job interview) or internal.

Stress is, therefore, an adaptive process with the following steps:

◇ The adverse changes in the environment are perceived by the brain regions, leading to release of stress mediator molecules to deal with the changes

◇ This triggers the stress responses in the person, including physiological, cognitive and behavioural responses, that enable the person to adapt to the stressful changes in the environment

1.3 Short-term stress

Stress can be useful in the short term. It is useful for functioning and survival, since it helps the body to be alert and deal with the immediate issue that needs attention. It helps the person to get an improved performance in terms of memory, alertness and other faculties.

For example, if we have an important work deadline or exam coming up, stress helps to focus the blood flow to focus on the brain and this helps us to think more clearly.

Therefore, in evolution, stress helped us to survive better by dealing with the imminent threat immediately.

1.4 Biological mechanisms of stress

The biological mechanisms of stress function in such a way that energy of the body and the blood gets diverted to the brain when the stressor (adverse change in environment) occurs, at the cost of longer term and less urgent mechanisms such as digestion, so that the person is better able to deal with the immediate threat or task. The body responds to stress in a dynamic and adaptive way, such as via increased heart rate and faster breathing and other appropriate changes. The result is that the stable function of the body is maintained.

The biological mechanisms of adaptation include things such as activation of the HPA axis (hypothalamic–pituitary–adrenal axis). This involves the activation of the region of the brain called hypothalamus, which then activates the pituitary glands and then affects the adrenal cortex activating the adrenal glands. The adrenal gland releases the hormone cortisol in the blood. This causes changes in the sympathetic nervous system, which governs the fight or flight response, causing changes such as pupil dilation, conversion of glycogen to glucose, secretion of adrenaline and noradrenaline, reduces the bladder constriction and digestive system, increases heart rate etc. It also causes changes in the immune system, cardiovascular system affecting blood pressure, and related changes, in such a way that one is better equipped to deal with the stressor. This normal adaptive response is termed as allostasis. Input from the amygdala region of the brain that deals with emotions is also involved in the HPA axis activation.

1.5 Chronic or long-term stress

In the long term, in modern day life, most of our stress is not caused by a sudden danger or threat. It is more of a continued low intensity stress such as fear of losing our job or financial troubles. This causes long term or chronic stress.

When we are under chronic stress, the benefits such as increased alertness that we get from short term stress no longer holds true. Repeated, prolonged or chronic stress can reduce the effectiveness of the normal allostatic response of the body. It can weaken our immune system, cause health conditions such as diabetes and significantly weaken our standard of life. It impacts our wellbeing and our cognitive performance.

This detrimental cumulative effect of chronic stress is termed as allostatic load.

A good overview of how stress works can be found in the following book: Sapolsky, R. M. (2004). Why zebras don't get ulcers: The acclaimed guide to stress, stress-related diseases, and coping. Holt paperbacks.

1.6 Introduction to Mindfulness

Mindfulness, or mindful meditation, such as the ones taught in structured programs like MBSR or mindfulness-based stress reduction, can help to reduce the stress.

Mindfulness is all about calming the mind and paying attention to whatever is in front of us at any moment. The object of attention can vary from the breath, body postures or activities like walking, running or exercise, daily activities like washing the dishes, and so on. The main point is to not let the mind wander off or distracted in a chain of thoughts, but to keep it in the present moment. It can be practiced as a sitting meditation at certain times in the day or applied in smaller chunks within daily life.

Mindfulness involves exercises such as sitting in a meditation posture (back erect, cross legged, closed eyes, hands on lap) and paying attention to the breath as it comes in an goes out through the nostrils. One pays gentle and sustained focused attention on the breath. If the mind wanders, such as a thought occurs or an itch or pain sensation occurs, one acknowledges the sensation, notes it (one can use a neutral word such as pain, pain or thinking, thinking) and gently returns to noting the breath. One does not need to go deeper into the sensations, but if any movement is needed to get rid of something like pain in the leg, that is done also very slowly and mindfully.

Here, it is important to clarify that mindfulness is not the same as focus or concentration. Focus means paying attention only to one thing in front of our mind. But usually, when working in front of a computer, we may have things like a little bit of back pain because of posture, a few thoughts of anger or irritation, some stress or worry, shallow breathing, feeling of sadness etc, all at the same time. Mostly we do not notice all these little sensations and feelings. Mindfulness is paying attention to all of these one by one, but not getting fixated on any one. And although mindfulness is not the same as focus, making a habit of being mindful can actually help us to focus better because our tendency to have too many wandering thoughts would decrease once we make a habit of staying mindful.

Mindfulness has been found to be therapeutic and useful in helping people deal with a variety of mental and physical ailments. There are also side benefits of mindfulness such as increased focus, productivity and an enhanced feeling of well-being and happiness.

1.7 Mindfulness for stress reduction

The mechanism how mindfulness can help reduce stress is by training us to note our body sensations as they occur and thus increase our awareness of the stress response. It also trains us to accept our thoughts and feelings as they occur, without judging them as desirable or not.

The beneficial effects of mindfulness on stress have been studied widely. Mindfulness helps to enhance the immune system and other mechanisms. Biological markers of stress such as the cortisol levels in saliva and blood, blood pressure, heart rate variability, cytokine levels, and so on have been measured in various studies and found to be improved in case of practitioners who have done the MBSR course, compared with control groups without MBSR.

Some important books and articles by Jon Kabat Zinn explaining MBSR are as follows:

◈ Kabat-Zinn, J. (1994). Wherever you go, there you are: Mindfulness meditation in everyday life. New York: Hyperion.

◈ Kabat-Zinn, J. (2013). Full catastrophe living, revised edition: how to cope with stress, pain and illness using mindfulness meditation. Hachette UK.

◈ Kabat-Zinn, J. (2013). Some reflections on the origins of MBSR, skillful means, and the trouble with maps. Mindfulness (pp. 281–306). Routledge.

In the area of technology too, application of mindfulness can lead to a number of benefits and prevent or slow down the physical or mental issues that may arise when using technology.

1.8 Ways to use mindfulness while using tech gadgets

In this section, we look at some practical ways in which mindfulness can be used when using a computer or any other gadget.

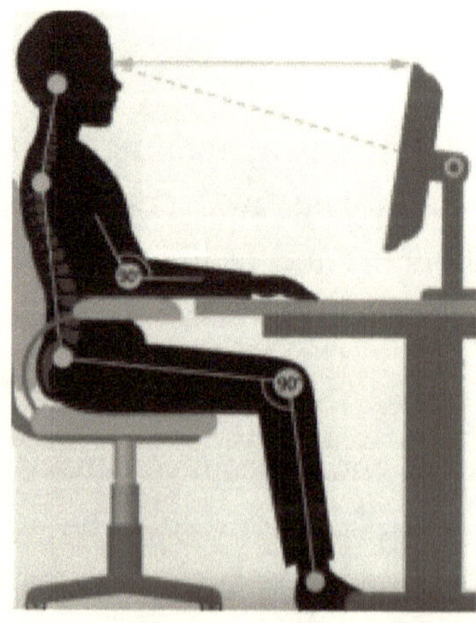

Figure: An example of a correct sitting posture

◇ **Be mindful of posture**: The idea here is to remind ourselves periodically to be mindful of our posture when using the tech gadgets, be it TV, mobile or a laptop. While using a laptop, this could include having a straight back, eyes, hands and fingers at the recommended angles.

◇ **Be mindful of breathing**: We can set ourselves occasional reminders to breathe more slowly and deeply. slow and deep breathing is good for our health and for relaxation, while shallow and faster breathing are signs of stress.

◇ **Be mindful of taking short breaks**: Short breaks (say once an hour) are vital when using tech. We should remind ourselves to take a short walk, maybe get a cup of tea or glass of water, once every hour at least. That is useful for reducing strain on our eyes, besides others.

◇ **Be mindful of the state of our mind when consuming content using tech**: Sometimes we tend to get carried away and get too absorbed in the work we are doing when using tech. It may be helpful here to be mindful of our thoughts from time to time, also to be mindful of what content (such as news or social media feeds) we are consuming.

◇ **Be mindful on how we interact with others using tech**: Often we are on autopilot and have no time to look back and be mindful of how we interact with others or what is the impact on our minds when we are receiving, creating or interacting with online content. We may for example, send off an angry email or reply to a social media post in a rude way, something we may regret later. So it might be worthwhile to consider how our content will affect other people and be mindful of their feelings too.

◇ **Control the notifications on your mobile and popups on PC**: Constant notifications are a cause of distraction and irritation, so it is a good idea to control or disable unnecessary notifications and/ or popups. The website technology for mindfulness (https://technologyformindfulness.com/) offers a number of useful tips for increasing mindfulness and avoiding distractions.

1.9 Ways to plan our day mindfully

Even when we are not using tech gadgets (before and after using them) we can plan our day mindfully, so as to reduce the adverse impact of using the gadgets. Examples of this can be as follows:

◇ **Mindfully stick to a schedule**: This could be as simple as sleeping and waking up at fixed hours and consciously making time for three meals. It could also include being mindful of what we eat and drink, whether we are having a balanced diet etc.

◇ **Plan a mindfulness meditation in the morning or during the day**: This could mean setting aside a fixed time, say 15–20 minutes, for a mindfulness meditation session.

◇ **Mindfully plan and recollect your day as a whole**: This is simply remembering how the day went by, what we learnt from it before we go to sleep. It can also include spending a few moments planning how we want our day to go before we jump out of bed in the morning.

◇ **Set boundaries around tech usage**: We can set some time or space boundaries around our usage of tech. For example, we can decide not to touch or use any tech gadgets after 10 pm and before 4 am, or when we are visiting a specific room in our house.

1.10 Ways to use technology to enhance our mindfulness

Technology can also be used in a positive way, to enhance our mindfulness and well-being during the day. Some of the ways it can help are as follows:

Figure: Popular mindfulness meditation apps

Using mindfulness apps to meditate: There are a number of good mindfulness and meditation apps on the google play store or app store that can help us to do mindfulness meditation.

Examples of mindfulness apps include the following:

⬦ Calm. https://www.calm.com/

⬦ Insight Timer https://insighttimer.com/

⬦ The Mindfulness App. https://themindfulnessapp.com/

⬦ Stop, Breathe and Think. https://my.life/

⬦ Headspace. https://www.headspace.com/

⬦ Buddhify. https://buddhify.com/

The plum village website (https://plumvillage.org/mindfulness-practice/mindful-apps/) has a good number of useful links to mindful apps and related software.

However, it can become a problem if we install too many mindfulness apps! Therefore, it is better to try them out, choose a few (maximum 4 or 5) that we like best, then uninstall the other apps.

Using a mindfulness bell: The concept of a mindfulness bell to 'wake us' up to the present moment was introduced by a famous Vietnamese teacher called Thich Nhat Hanh.

Some apps and websites related to mindfulness bell are as follows:

⬦ Awakening bell website. https://awakeningbell.org/

⬦ Bell of Mindfulness Chrome browser extension (https://chrome.google.com/webstore/detail/bell-of-mindfulness/lggmmceliiaoddfnbaccgpfnpoifilic) that will ring a bell or gong at the time intervals we specify.

Such a bell can be used as a trigger for ourselves to bring our mind back to the present moment.

Creativity enhancing apps: Examples can include mindfulness colouring apps, which can be searched on the Google play store or apple app store. While using such colouring apps, our mindfulness can be cultivated since we are focused on colouring and not distracted by thoughts.

Mindfulness enhancing games: Some PC games can be used to enhance mindfulness. Some of these games include the following

⬦ Just Sleep PC game

⬦ Playne PC game

⬦ Flow Playstation 4 game

⬦ Mindfulness games available on mobile (android/iOS) include Forest and PAUSE

Using gadgets and wearables to be mindful: There are some gadgets or wearables that can help us to meditate better and be more mindful. We will go through them in detail in later chapters, but here we give a brief overview of such gadgets.

Examples of mindfulness gadgets include EEG headsets such as Neurosky and Muse. EEG headsets use electroencephalography or EEG to create a feedback loop to understand how much relaxed we are while meditating. Other gadgets measure our heart rate and breathing, to get an idea of how relaxed or stressed we are during the day. An example is spire stone. Also, most fitness trackers and smartwatches usually have a heart rate and breath tracking function in it. Using this, we can track how was our breath rate and heart rate, along with how many steps we walked etc.

Setting reminders to be mindful: We can set periodic reminders to be mindful of our breathing, posture or taking a break, on our computer or mobile phone, using software such as outlook, task scheduler on Windows or dedicated apps. Browser extensions such as Bell of Mindfulness and StayFocusd (a browser extension that blocks distracting websites, https://chrome.google.com/webstore/detail/stayfocusd-block-distract/laankejkbhbdhmipfmgcngdelahlfoji), can also be helpful in this. We can also set our desktop and screensaver to something that reminds us to be mindful. We can use all such reminders as a cue to bring back our mind to the present moment.

Listening to mindfulness sounds and music: This can be as simple as including in our playlist some sounds that enhance being in the present moment in nature, such as sounds of rain, sound of waves, sounds of birds chirping etc. Mindfulness enhancing music, such as binaural beats, chanting sounds, or classical music such as Mozart or Hindustani classical or Chinese classical music, can also be of help to some.

1.11 Conclusion

In this chapter we discussed an overview of how we can enhance our mindfulness while using technology during our day, and also how to use tech as a tool to improve our mindfulness. Using some of these ways, we can cultivate mindfulness as a skill and use it to enhance our well-being. In the following chapters, we will go through some of these gadgets and apps in more detail.

Chapter 2: Breath monitoring in Smartwatches and fitness bands

Figure: Smartwatch. Photo by Andres Urena on Unsplash

Apple watch, Fitbit Charge, Samsung Gear fit, Mi fit, Moov now are some of the fitness bands and watches available in the market, that have the ability to monitor the user's pulse rate. Some of these, though not all, have apps that can help the user to relax.

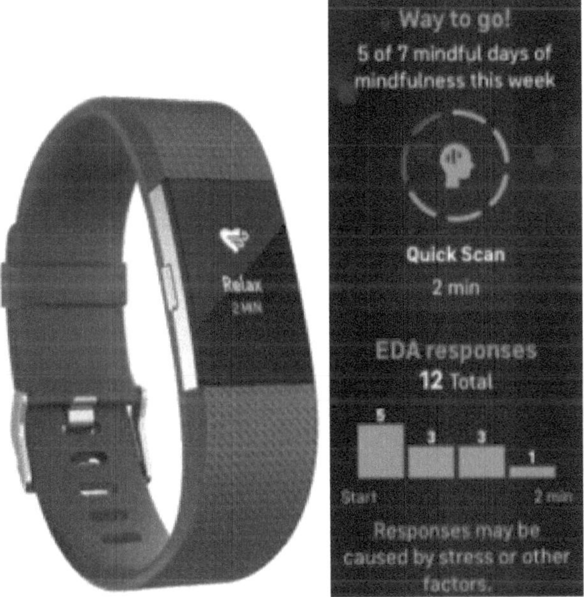

Figure: Fitbit Relax smartband, and tracking mindfulness sessions using Fitbit relax

Fitbit's relax is one such app. It is available on a number of Fitbit devices including Blaze, Charge, Inspire and Sense. It has guided meditation sessions, including mindfulness meditation, to help the user to relax. The Fitbit can also track one's stress throughout the day.

Chapter 3: Wearable gadget based on biofeedback: Unyte IOM2

In this chapter, we discuss a wearable gadget based on biofeedback, called Unyte IOM2. It tracks the breathing rhythm of the participants and uses it in beautiful PC and mobile based games to train the participant to be more relaxed by breathing more deeply.

3.1 Introduction to biofeedback

Biofeedback refers to completing a loop, with the person wearing a wearable gadget giving feedback (in terms of changes in breathing, pulse rate, brain waves or EEG and so on) that helps to further tune the behavior of the wearable gadget or device. The breathing, pulse rate, skin conductance measurements are some of the things that can be measured easily by inexpensive sensors, and which can give an indication as to how relaxed or stressed a person is.

3.2 Introduction to Unyte IOM2

An example of a biofeedback-based biosensor is the relaxation game based software from WildDivine (now called Unyte) such as Unyte IOM2, which uses a sensor for breathing rate and pulse rate to trigger different actions in a variety of games, with the aim of scoring more points as the person relaxes and the pulse rate becomes slower.

The Unyte IOM2 is a meditation and relaxation biofeedback device. It measures the Heart Rate variability and combines with PC and Android/IOS based relaxation exercises while measuring the heart rate variability of HRV signals in real time.

Unyte IOM2 is a full cycle biofeedback device: Unlike many other such devices, it not only measures the bio-signals (heart rate variability as we breathe in and out) but also combines with web based or PC based games that respond to our breathing, with the sensors sending signals to the game. For example, the game may have balloons which expand or contract with our breathing in and out: if we breathe more slowly it may expand more slowly and get more points etc. At the end of the game, it is designed to make us more relaxed.

One can read more details at https://integratedlistening.com/iom2/ and https://wilddivine.com/pages/iom2

3.3 How to get the Unyte IOM2

To use the device and its accompanying software, one needs to purchase the device with a subscription.

One can buy the device either from Amazon (search Amazon for Unyte IOM2) or from the Untye IOM webpage https://wilddivine.com/pages/iom2. We can click on the "Order Now" button on the webpage.

The device cost is between $130-$140 and the subscription cost is $59 a year or about $259 for lifetime.

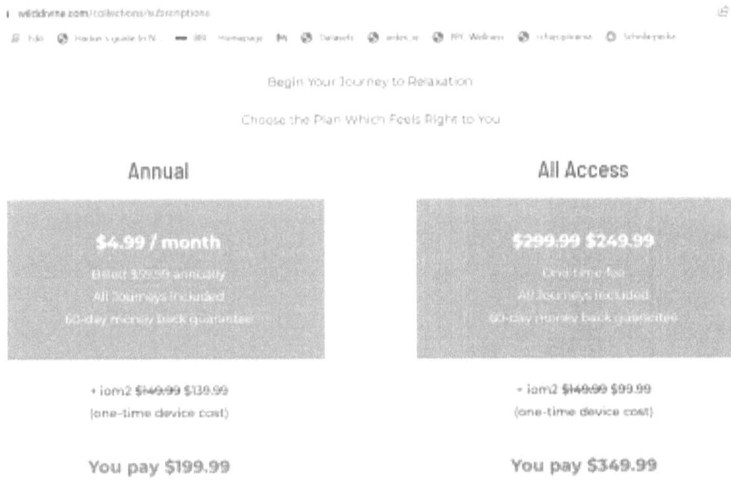

Figure: Bundled Subscription plans for buying the Unyte IOM2 device with subscription (costs as of August 2022)

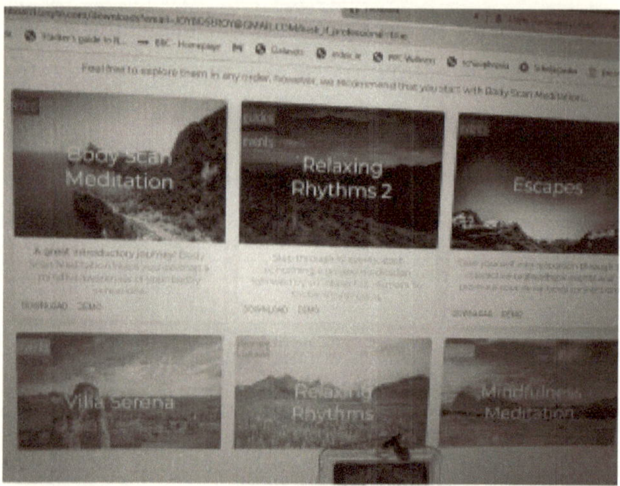

Figure: Different meditation/relaxation games available that are paired with the device and that one can download from the UNYTE IOM2 website

After purchasing a subscription, one can log in to their website and download the PC based meditation games.

There are a huge variety of meditation games that one can download with the Unyte IOM2, ranging from relaxation games to zen to mindfulness and body scan. There are Zen teachings by a zen monk, teachings by Thich Nhat Hanh, mindfulness meditation by Tara Brach and meditation by many other teachers.

Figure: The box containing the Unyte IOM2 device

3.4 Unboxing and setting up the Unyte IOM2 device

For setting up the device, one needs to connect the USB cable to the computer which has the software downloaded and installed from the website already.

One also needs to clip the sensor to the ear, while the other end of the sensor is connected to the device.

A Bluetooth connection option is also available, which is useful if the game is installed as an app on the mobile phone.

Figure: The Unyte IOM2 device along with accessories. Accessories include a USB cord and the sensor that is to be clipped to one's ear

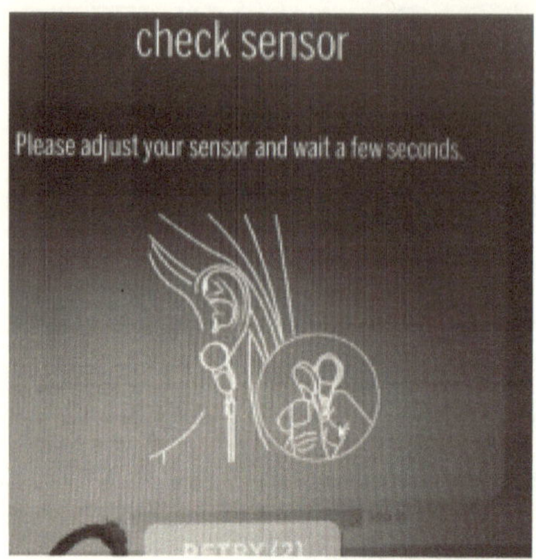

Figure: Message when setting up the Unyte IOM2 sensor

The device includes a biofeedback sensor which one can clip to one's ear. It can sense the breathing in and out.

Figure: The Unyte IOM2 sensor clipped to one's ear

Once the sensor is connected, one can see one's heart rate variability plotted across time, as well as the resonance score. The games software has the interface to show these values.

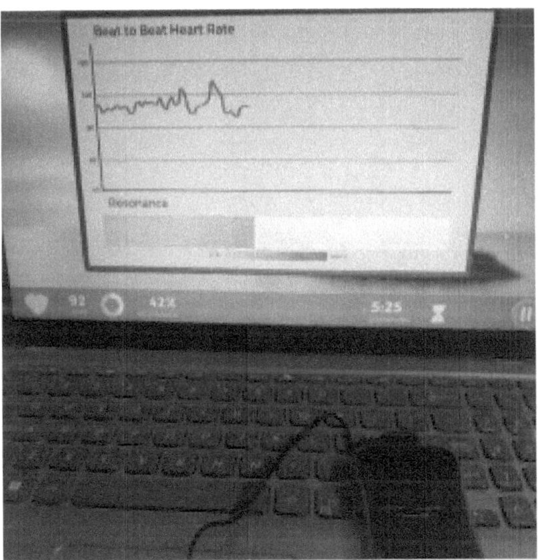

Figure: Chart of the heart rate with time when one is playing the meditation game with the sensor clipped to the ear

Figure: Interface for the PC game for the Unyte IOM2, with the sensor being connected to the PC or laptop via USB.

There is an online dashboard at https://dashboard.unyte.com/ where one can log in and see the HRV and other scores so far.

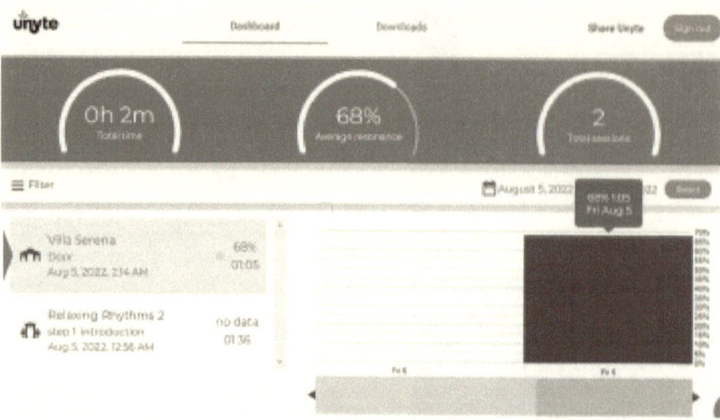

Figure: Web based dashboard for Unyte IOM2, which gives the total time spent in doing the exercises, average heart rate and resonance

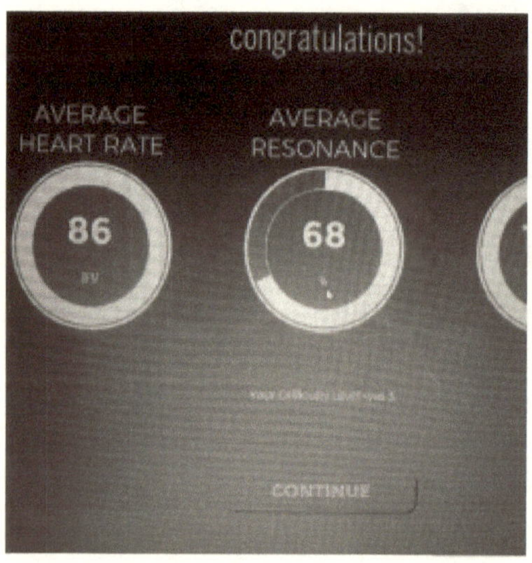

Figure: Dashboard after one has played a meditation game on Unyte IOM2, showing the performance in terms of average heart rate and resonance.

Figure: The interface for one of the meditation/ relaxation games on the Unyte IOM2

3.5 How the meditation and relaxation games work with Unyte IOM2

The basic idea in Unyte IOM2 is to train one to do deep breathing meditation and thus become more relaxed. The device can sense when we are breathing in and out. There is a measure called "resonance" which is about how well our breathing is synchronized by the breathing suggested during the game via an indicator which shows when to breathe in or out. The higher the resonance score, the more points one can get and advance to the next level in the game.

The meditation/relaxation games are available for the subscribed users on the PC as well as mobile. The games are to be played with the device connected using USB in case of PC, and Bluetooth in case of mobile phone.

At the end of the game, it shows the average heart rate and resonance during that game. The higher the resonance score, the better it is.

Figure: Android app screen for one of the games. The same games can be installed both on the PC and mobile phone

3.6 Android / IOS App Screens for the Unyte IOM2 meditation games

The android/IOS apps for Unyte IOM2 has screens similar to the PC games software screens.

3.7 Conclusion

In this chapter we have gone through the Unyte IOM2 biofeedback device and how to use it. This is an amazing device, different from other meditation gadgets in the market, since it completes the biofeedback cycle by using the breathing to advance in the meditation games.

Chapter 4: Wearable gadgets based on Electroencephalography (EEG)

In this chapter, we discuss EEG technology and some EEG headsets commercially available in the market, which can be used to help in meditation, using neurofeedback.

4.1 What is Electroencephalography or EEG

The definition of EEG from Wikipedia is as follows:

Electroencephalography (EEG) is a method to record an electrogram of the spontaneous electrical activity of the brain. The biosignals detected by EEG have been shown to represent the postsynaptic potentials of pyramidal neurons in the neocortex and allocortex.

Therefore, EEG is a technology that gives the aggregate activity of the neurons in the brain, as measured by one or multiple EEG sensors worn on the head by the subject and which take the recording of the brain activity from the scalp. It records the activity of the brain waves oscillating at various frequencies. It is non-invasive and easy to use, cheap and has a fast temporal resolution, meaning it can capture the activity in almost real time, although it has drawbacks such as low spatial resolution. While other brain imaging techniques such as FMRI, MEG and PET also exist, EEG has been the most successful brain imaging technique commercially and the general public due to its ease of use and low cost of devices.

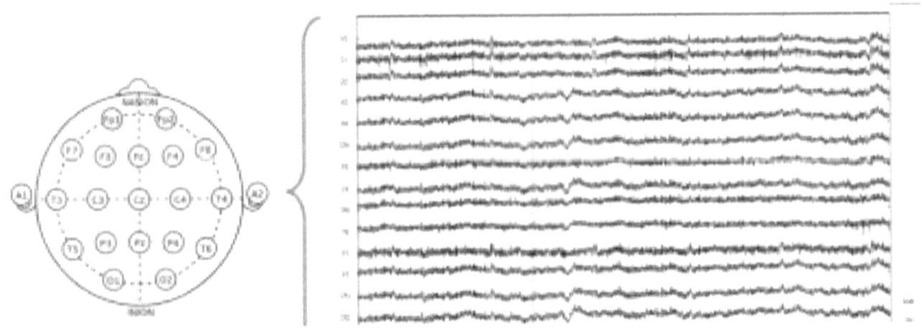

Figure: EEG recording (right) from electrodes fitted in the subject's head (left)

4.2 How do EEG gadgets work

EEG based gadgets work on the principle of neurofeedback, by receiving the EEG signals on a connected wearable gadget and performing various tasks in response to the variations in the subject's brain activity.

Neurofeedback is the similar to biofeedback, but applied to neural signals from the brain measured by EEG or electroencephalography sensors. One can measure different kinds of EEG signals such as alpha and gamma that correlate with concentration, meditation, and deep sleep.

The EEG signals are communicated via Bluetooth to a connected smartphone, and the apps build on top of it.

Commercial grade EEG kits and wearables are a fast-growing field, since EEG is scientifically proven, safe and has a number of relatively inexpensive wearable gadgets available in the market. Many of these wearables have available APIs to enable developers to create their own apps and games based on the EEG signals.

4.3 Popular commercially sold EEG wearable gadgets

Some of the popular wearables based on EEG are as follows:

- Emotiv Insight (https://www.emotiv.com/insight/)

- Neurosky Mindwave (https://store.neurosky.com/pages/mindwave)

- Muse Headband (https://choosemuse.com/)

- Brainlink

- OpenBCI EEG headband (https://shop.openbci.com/products/openbci-eeg-headband-kit)

- Neuphony (https://neuphony.com/)

◈ Necomimi (https://necomimi.shop/en)

Each of the above gadgets come with a range of EEG based apps and games in the google play store and apple app store.

A number of other EEG based sensors are in development, being funded on kickstarter etc, or are entering the market.

In the following sections, we shall discuss the authors' experience of using some of these gadgets in more detail.

Figure: Neurosky EEG headset. The sensor is put on the forehead and the rest of the headset fits around the head. It is quite lightweight. The clip is put on the earlobe.

Figure: Person wearing the Neurosky EEG headset

4.4 Experience with using Neurosky Mindwave

The Neurosky Mindwave EEG wearable gadget has just one EEG sensor placed on the forehead, is very lightweight and looks and feels like a headphone. It is the cheapest (or one of the cheapest) EEG based wearable available in the market and has a number of Android and IOS Apps and games, including apps to track how well the meditation session went.

Cost of Neurosky Mindwave headset

One can buy the headset for only Indian Rupees 12000 from Amazon India.

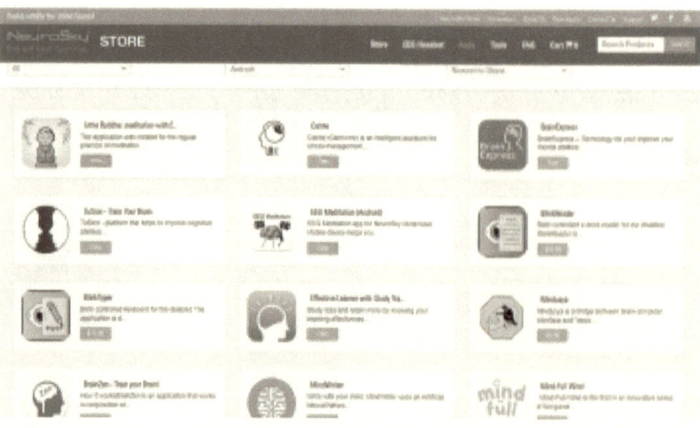

Figure: Screenshot of the Neurosky web store showing the available apps with Neurosky EEG headset

Connected apps with the Neurosky Mindwave on the web store

There are dozens of connected apps for Neurosky that one can download from Android play store or from the neurosky website.

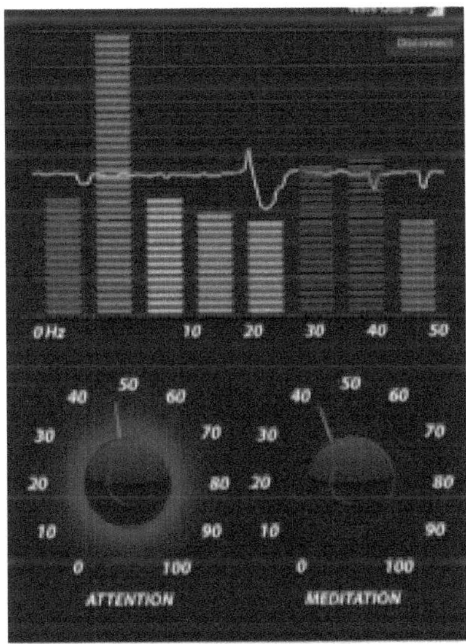

Figure: Screenshot of the Neurosky Brainwave visualizer app

How to use Neurosky Mindwave

The Neurosky Mindwave gadget is likewise paired with the phone and communicates with the phone via Bluetooth. It gives a relaxation score and a meditation score in real time on the connected app called Brainwave Visualizer, that one can download from the Google play store or the Apple app store.

One can do meditation with the Neurosky Mindwave, as well as play a number of games available on their web store.

Problems with Neurosky Mindwave

However, Neurosky has only one sensor and has a delay in reporting changed brain state to the connected app. Also, it's meditation reading wasn't all that accurate when I tried it, but maybe they improved it in the later versions.

4.5 Experience with using Muse headband

Muse is a meditation headset that takes the EEG signals and transmits it via Bluetooth to the mobile phone. Of the existing commercial grade EEG gadgets, Muse is the device most optimized for meditation. Muse has a number of guided meditations in its accompanying app and is based on a subscription-based model. The original Muse only has EEG sensors, while Muse 2 uses a range of body sensors including EEG, pulse, heart rate and breathing to give a more holistic guidance for meditation and relaxation.

Figure: Unboxing the Muse EEG Gadget

Cost of Muse EEG headset

Muse costs $149 for the older version plus free delivery, for delivery to India from USA. The latest version costs $249.

To this we must also add the India customs fees of around Rupees 6000 in order to import it to India.

Figure: Screenshot of the Muse app, which accompanies the Muse and Muse 2 wearable gadgets. It has a few guided meditations one can use.

Figure: Graph plotted on the Muse app after a meditation session with the Muse EEG wearable gadget.

Author's feedback on meditating with Muse

The author has had some experience with meditating with the Muse headset.

Muse seems to be quite accurate in assessing the quality of the meditation session and even has a feedback component.

It has a connected app that does a guided meditation. If your mind is wandering during the meditation session while wearing the Muse connected to your phone and its associated app, you will hear the sound of thunder.

If during the meditation session with the Muse and its connected app, your mind is concentrated on the breath, you will hear a bird chirp in the connected app. This real time sound feedback that we get during the meditation session helps us to control the wandering mind and learn the skill of focusing on the breath and relax deeply.

The connected app with Muse shows the results of a short guided meditation session. It shows exactly for how many seconds during the session we got a good meditation, number of seconds we were in a neutral state, and number of seconds we were distracted.

At the end of the meditation session, we get an overall report how the meditation session went.

Overall, the authors found Muse to be one of the best gadgets available for improving the meditation practice.

Figure: Brainlink EEG gadget

4.6 Experience with using Brainlink

Like Muse and Neurosky, Brainlink is another wearable EEG gadget with a connected app on the Android phone.

Brainlink is a China built EEG gadget which is good for testing the quality of your meditation. It is also comparatively cheaper.

Figure: Screenshot from the connected app with the Brainlink EEG gadget after a meditation session. Connected app with Brainlink EEG wearable.

The connected app on the smartphone with Brainlink gives the user feedback on the quality of the meditation or relaxation session.

Figure: Emotiv Insight EEG gadget. Taken from https://www.emotiv.com/ product-category/mobile-eeg-headsets/

4.7 Experience with Emotiv EPOC

The Emotiv EEG headset is available in two varieties: EPOC and Insight. It claims to be the most accurate and research grade and has the most number of sensors, but is also a little pricier than the others.

The authors spent only a short time with Emotiv EPOC. It was the most accurate of the EEG headsets (compared to Neurosky and Muse) due to having highest number of sensors, a total of eight.

It also had the highest cost, $750 for a research license.

4.8 Conclusion

In this chapter, we have introduced EEG and discussed a few of the commercial grade EEG wearable gadgets available on the market. The field continues to advance rapidly. In 2025, InteraXon released the Muse S Athena, which combines EEG with functional near-infrared spectroscopy (fNIRS) in a single headband for the first time in a consumer device, offering richer and more accurate insights into both brain activity and cognitive effort. Another notable entrant, the Mendi headband, uses fNIRS alone (without EEG) and has been validated by research partners including Stanford and Princeton Universities. These and other next-generation gadgets are discussed further in Chapter 23.

Chapter 5: Meditation Smart Ring: Dhyana

In this chapter, we go discuss a smart ring called Dhyana, which is suitable for meditation. It is made in India and available on its own website as well as on Amazon.

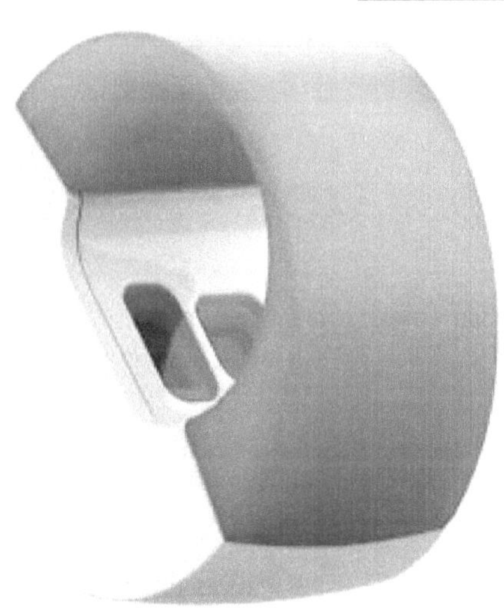

Figure: Dhyana smart ring

5.1 Introduction to wearables for measurement of stress levels

There are many smart rings and other wearables available that measure the stress level throughout the day. Some of them are as follows:

◈ Pip is a biofeedback device that monitors the conductance of the skin pores on the fingertips to get an idea of the amount of stress. The website is https://thepip.com/en-eu/

◈ Spire Stone is a wearable gadget that uses the breathing rate to measure and control the stress throughout the day. Its website is https://spirehealth.com/pages/stone

◈ Flo is a wearable gadget in the form of a necklace, that helps one to relieve stress by slowing down breathing. Its website is https://www.flomktg.com/work/innovative-wearable-technology

◈ Dhyana is a meditation ring, also based on biofeedback of the heart rate variability, that can measure how well one is meditating. The website is https://www.smartdhyana.com/

5.2 Heart Rate Variability or HRV

Dhyana smart ring meditation tracker works by measuring the heart rate variability (HRV) when a person is meditating. HRV measures the variation in time between heartbeats. Lower HRV is associated with a number of health conditions such as congestive heart failure and diabetic neuropathy. Another application of HRV is to measure meditation.

5.3 How Dhyana Smart Ring works

Dhyana smart ring gives an indication of how deep is the meditation, how slow is the rate of breathing, how much the subject was mindful of the breath and so on.

The smart ring is fitted on one of the fingers and measures HRV in perhaps as similar way as the pulse rate. It then sends the data to the dhyana app, freely downloadable from Google play store and apple app store.

The app is paired to the ring using bluetooth. Using the app, the user can then view the data, how well they were focused or mindful during the meditation session. The app contains a variety of guided meditations and also has features like reminder to start meditating at certain times of the day and for short time periods, like 5 or 10 minutes.

5.4 Ordering and unboxing Dhyana Smart Ring

The first step is to order the smart ring, either from the Dhyana website or for amazon. There is a discount available, the price after discount comes to about Indian Rs 5500 on Amazon India.

The packaging is quite compact and beautiful. There is also a booklet with instructions on how to use the Dhyana smart ring.

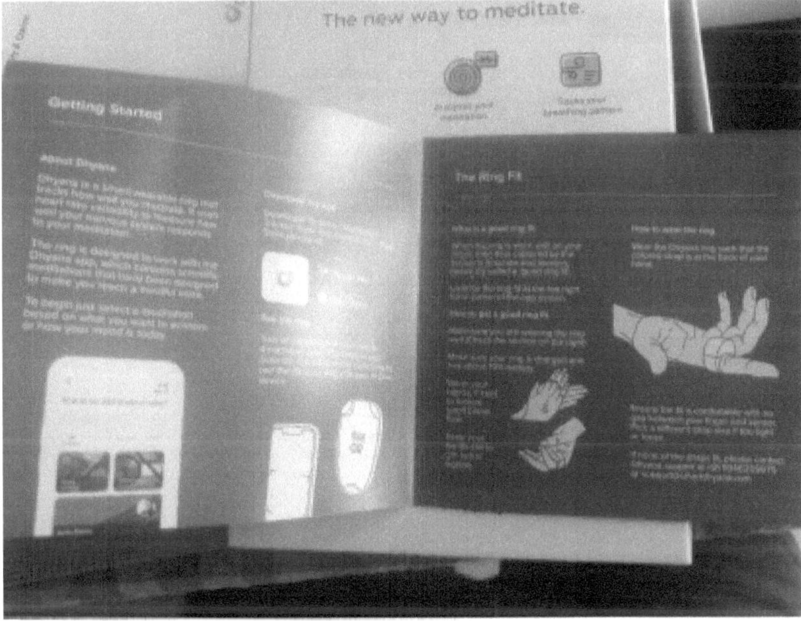

Figure: Unboxing the Dhyana Smart ring

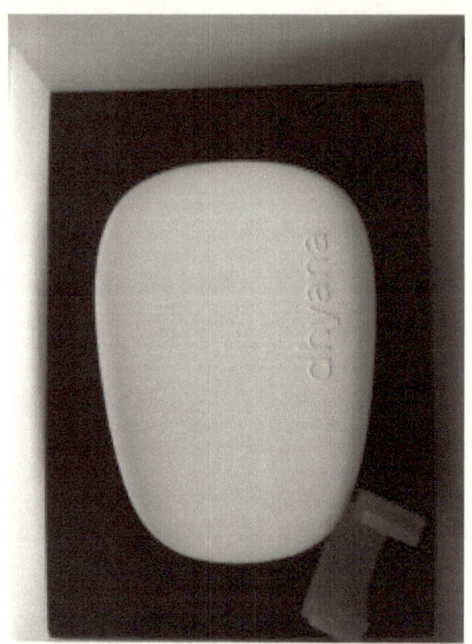

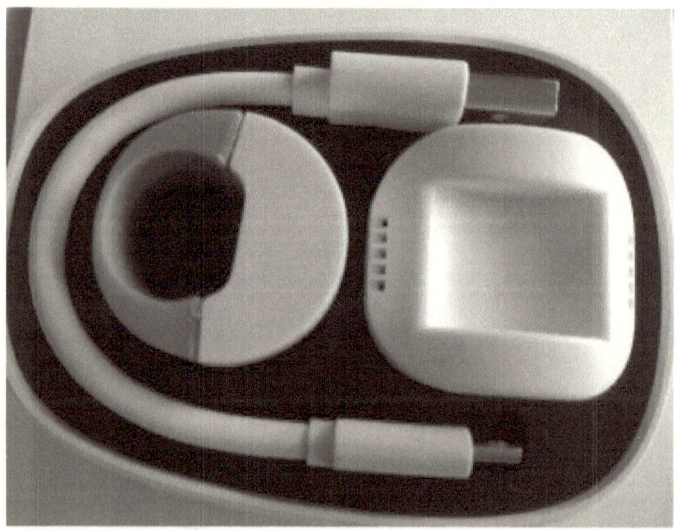

Figure: Unboxing the Dhyana smart ring along with its accessories

Figure: Charging the Dhyana smart ring using USB from the PC.

When it arrives, unbox it and charge the ring using the given USB charger from the box.

The colour will turn blue and stop flickering when it is fully charged.

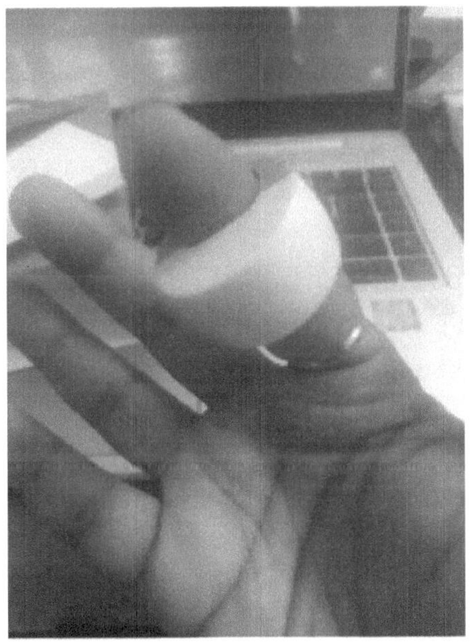

Figure: Fitting the Dhyana smart ring on one's finger before starting the meditation session

There are three straps of different sizes to fit the ring on the finger. Best is to select the strap that fits the user's finger.

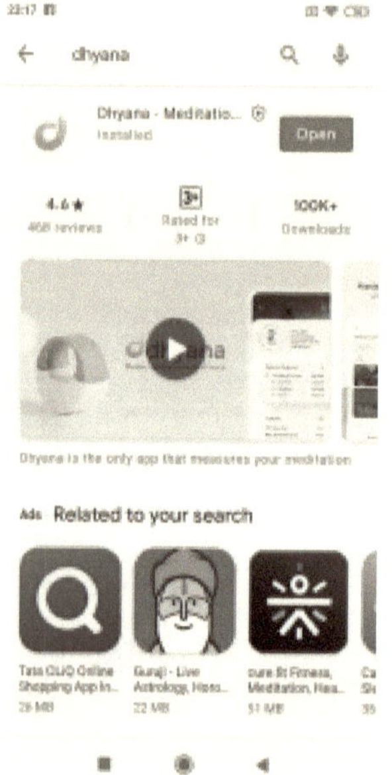

Figure: Dhyana app on Google play store

5.5 Downloading and using the Dhyana app

The next step is to download the Dhyana app from Google play store and pair the device to the app on the phone using Bluetooth.

The screenshots below show the app to be downloaded from the play store. The same app contains instructions on how to pair the device and how to fit it on the finger. One needs to create a (free) login on the app.

Once the pairing is done, the app contains a selection of guided meditations, with a range of times starting from as low as 3 to 5 minutes.

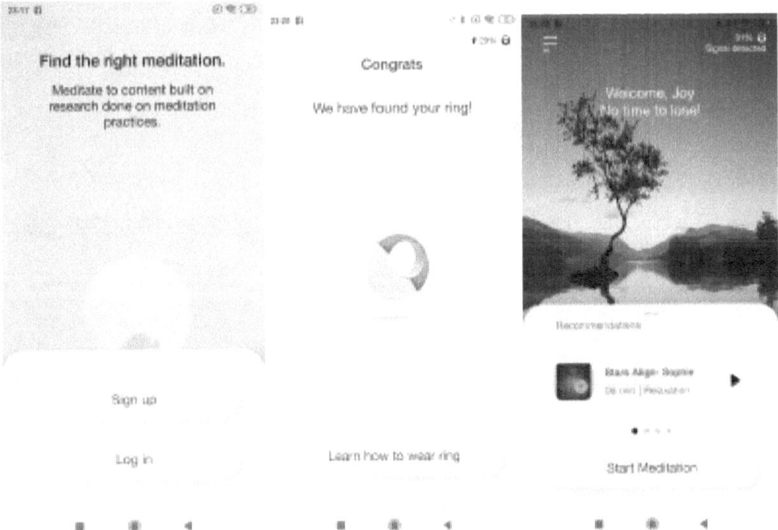

Figure: Screenshots from the Dhyana app on Android, showing the guided meditations

5.6 Guided meditations using the Dhyana app

The meditations contain instructions to breathe deeply in and out and also to be mindful and conscious of the breathing. There are also other meditations such as body scan, compassion and meditation for stress relief.

While one is following the meditation instructions on the app, the Dhyana smart ring is measuring the heart rate and whether it is synchronized with the instructions, indicating that the subject is paying attention.

Finally, at the end of the meditation session, the app gives a report of the stages of the meditation, how much time it was and how much of that time the person was being mindful.

Over a period of time of using the app, the quality of the meditation should improve.

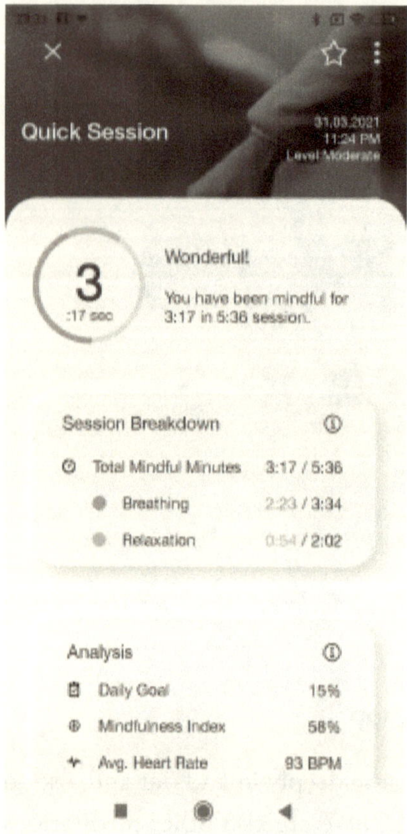

Figure: Report of a meditation session on the Dhyana app, indicating the quality of mindfulness meditation during the session.

5.7 Conclusion

The authors found the Dhyana app to be helpful in guiding beginners to meditation and also a nice and scientific objective way to keep track of how good the meditation session along with the smart ring is going.

Overall, Dhyana smart ring is a nice product that uses bio-feedback to track one's meditation, and also is relatively cheap compared to other such wearable devices available in the market.

Chapter 6: Wearables based on Transcranial Direct Current Stimulation (tDCS)

In this chapter we discuss a few wearable gadgets based on t-DCS technology.

6.1 What is tDCS and how do such devices work

Transcranial Direct Current Stimulation or tDCS is a method of stimulating a specific region of the brain with a small electric current (direct current) delivered via electrodes to the head of the subject. It can be used to enhance the subject's cognitive skills such as focus, as well as a treatment for certain mental conditions such as clinical depression. Due to its ease of use and wide applications, it has various medical and everyday uses, although their primary use is in the medical domain. Commercial versions of tDCS kits are now sold to help the subject to improve focus and other qualities.

Figure: Foc.us Go Flow wearable to stimulate the brain and increase focus based on tDCS

Our brain has certain areas which are responsible for different faculties like focus and emotion and which when stimulated, gives rise to the appropriate emotions. Transcranial direct current stimulation or t-DCS is a technology that gives a small electric current to certain areas of the brain that help in enhancing focus, calm or happiness, as the case may be depending on the area stimulated. It is a relatively new technology and has found to be generally safe to use.

The reddit page at https://www.reddit.com/r/tdcs/wiki/devices gives a list of how safe some of the popular tDCS devices are.

tDCS devices typically have one or more electrodes that are attached to parts of the head, and deliver a direct current. In some of the devices, the strength of the current and its duration can be customized by the user. After a certain amount of time for which the tDCS is delivered, the current is stopped, and the user can then engage in their regular tasks with an increased focus.

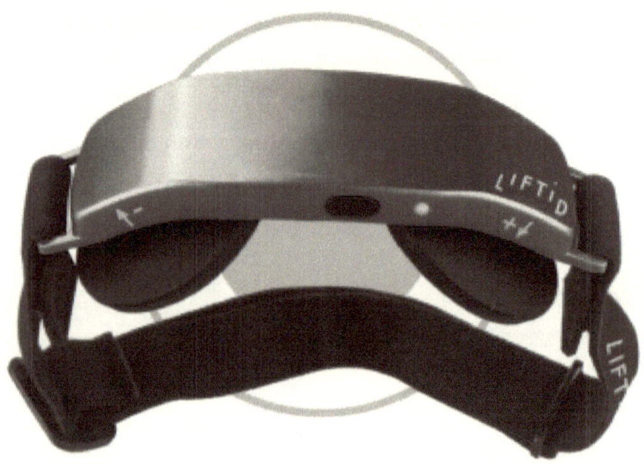

Figure: LIFTiD neurostimulation device based on tDCS

6.2 Commercial tDCS kits

Some of the commercially available tDCS devices are as follows:

◇ Thync is one of the tDCS wearables focused on enhancing calm and energy, and comes with an app that lets one choose the mood they want. The website is https://www.thync.com/

◇ Foc.us Go Flow brain stimulator is meant for enhancing focus of the subject. It delivers current up to 4 milliamperes. The website is https://foc.us/

◈ LIFTiD is another neurostimulation device based on tDCS technology, that increases focus. The website is https://www.getliftid.com/

6.3 Conclusion

In this chapter, we have discussed a few commercial kits based on tDCS technology, that can enhance focus in the subject.

Chapter 7: Wearable to stimulate mystical experience: Shiva helmet or God helmet

The Shiva helmet is also called Koren helmet, God helmet or Shiva neural transmission system.

It is a helmet based apparatus that applies magnetic signals to the brain's temporal lobes to stimulate mystical experiences.

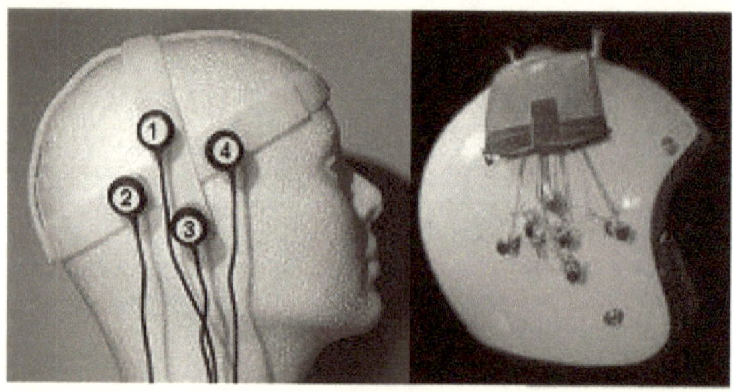

Figure: Shiva helmet or God helmet

The subject wears a helmet, and the magnetic signals are delivered through the helmet in the form of a rotating magnetic field. The technology was first invented by Dr. Michael Persinger.

Its website is https://www.god-helmet.com/wp/god-helmet/koren_understanding.htm

The same website from where one can order the helmet, also contains a few studies about studies on the efficacy of the helmet.

Chapter 8: Wearables to enhance lucid dreaming

In this chapter, we discuss some wearable gadgets related to lucid dreaming.

8.1 What is lucid dreaming and how do lucid dreaming gadgets work

Lucid dreaming refers to the state where the subject is aware they are dreaming in the midst of the dream. A subject in such a state can let their imagination run wild and do things they would not be able to do in waking state, such as fly. Therefore, it is an extraordinary experience, and is considered a form of meditation in some eastern traditions such as Buddhism and Hinduism.

There are some wearables that claim to make it easier to facilitate the lucid dreaming state. They consist of an EEG sensor to sense when the subject is entering the REM stage of sleep which is conducive to lucid dreaming, and then apply various means like give external stimuli (lights, sounds, or tiny electric currents) to enhance the probability of the lucid state.

An IEEE spectrum article, found at https://spectrum.ieee.org/tech-for-lucid-dreaming-takes-off-but-will-any-of-it-work discusses the science in more detail.

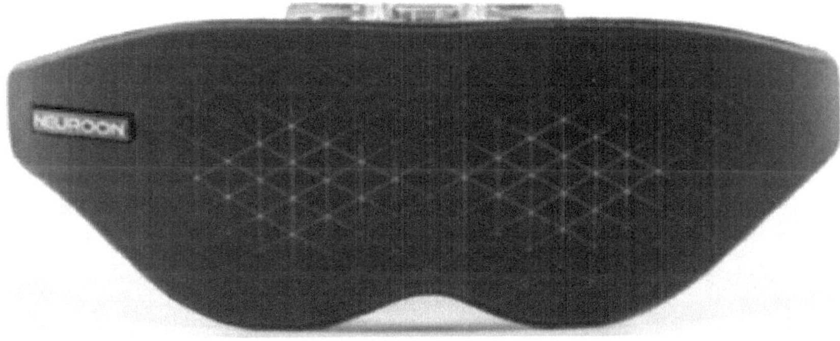

Figure: Neuroon sleep mask

8.2 Wearable gadgets related to lucid dreaming

Some of the wearable gadgets related to enhancing lucid dreaming include the following:

⬦ Neuroon open sleep tracker. This uses EEG technology along with guided meditations, to track and improve one's sleep. The website is https://www.kickstarter.com/projects/intelclinic/neuroon-open-smartest-sleep-dreams-and-meditation

⬦ Lucidcatcher. This is based on tACS technology, similar to tDCS. The website is https://www.kickstarter.com/projects/luciding/lucidcatcher-real-benefits-from-dreams

Both of the above are currently kickstarter projects, but it is hoped that full fledged commercial gadgets for lucid dreaming will soon become available.

8.3 Conclusion

In this chapter, we have discussed a few wearable gadgets related to enhancing the subject's lucid dreaming experience.

Chapter 9: Meditation lamps

Figure: Breathe meditation lamp

Meditation lamps are devices that act as a visual aid by giving fluctuating lights in relaxing colors to synchronize with breathing.

Breathe is an example of a meditation lamp that acts as a visual meditation aid for rhythmic breathing.

Its website is https://thegadgetflow.com/portfolio/breathe-the-meditation-lamp/

Chapter 10: Meditation apps

In this chapter, we discuss some of the meditation related apps that are available from the apple app store or the google play store. These are apps that are familiar to the authors and which they have personally used. There are many other meditation apps as well that can be searched and used.

Figure: Screenshot from the Headspace app

10.1 Introduction to meditation apps

A number of meditation and mindfulness apps are available on the google play store and apple app store. Some are free, some work on a freemium or subscription-based model, and give a range of guided meditations that help the user to relax.

These apps are mostly based on someone giving meditation instructions through the smartphone app. The user can customize the types of meditation (such as mindfulness, loving kindness, insight, concentration, zen, yoga, etc), time of the session and other parameters in these apps. Some of the apps have progressive levels of meditation, gamifying the experience to encourage the user to pick up the skill and be adept in meditation in a relatively short time.

Some of the popular mobile meditation apps related specifically to mindfulness meditation include the following:

- Headspace. The website is https://www.headspace.com/

- Calm. The website is https://www.calm.com/

- Insight timer. The website is https://insighttimer.com/

- Buddhify. The website is https://buddhify.com/

- The mindfulness app. The website is https://www.themindfulnessapp.com/

The writers of Headspace, Calm and Buddhify have related meditation books that one can buy on Amazon. These books explain the meditation in more detail.

There are also a few Yoga and Tai chi based apps available in the google play or apple store.

10.2 Android Apps for Mindfulness and Meditation

There are a huge number of mindfulness related Android apps including Smiling Mind, Medito, Omvana, Bliss, Mindfulness App, MyLife, Reimagining the Examen, Buddhify, Calm, Stop Breathe and Think, Waking Up. Another three are Headspace, Buddhify and Calm.

Most of these apps have various forms of timed and guided meditations.

A few details of the apps are as follows:

◇ Mindfulness App. This app contains a number of guided meditations including sitting meditation, walking meditation and compassion meditation.

◇ Plum Village App: this is based on Plum Village meditations led by the respected Vietnamese Buddhist master Thich Nhat Hanh, who recently passed away. It contains many guided meditations on mindfulness of breathing.

◇ MyLife app. When using this app, the subject has to pick their current state of mind and emotions for the day and on the basis of it, the app suggests a suitable meditation. This is very good for beginners to meditation.

◇ Mindfulness app, from UMass Memorial health Care Center for Mindfulness. This app contains many useful tips and advice about meditation.

◇ Smiling mind app. This is good for beginners, and contains an introduction to meditation and its types, as well as specific meditation instructions.

◇ Insight Timer app. It has a huge range of mindfulness meditations covering all aspects of mind and self-improvement. Also has a huge community participation, where one can meditate with other people. Insight Timer app. It also has the facility for the traditional meditation with bell and timer.

◇ Waking Up app by the famous neuroscientist Sam Harris. This explains the process of meditation in a very logical way.

◇ MyLife App: This too is suitable for beginners to meditation, and has a very friendly user interface.

◈ Headspace: This is a partly paid app and contains a structured program to help the user to become a good meditator over a period of time by following the program.

◈ Calm: This has a variety of meditations including meditations with natural relaxing sounds such as the sound of a beach and sound of rain.

◈ Buddhify: This has a number of mindfulness meditations suitable for busy people on the go or those who are traveling or in the gym etc. The user can select what type of meditation they want and what is their current mood, and the app can suggest suitable meditations.

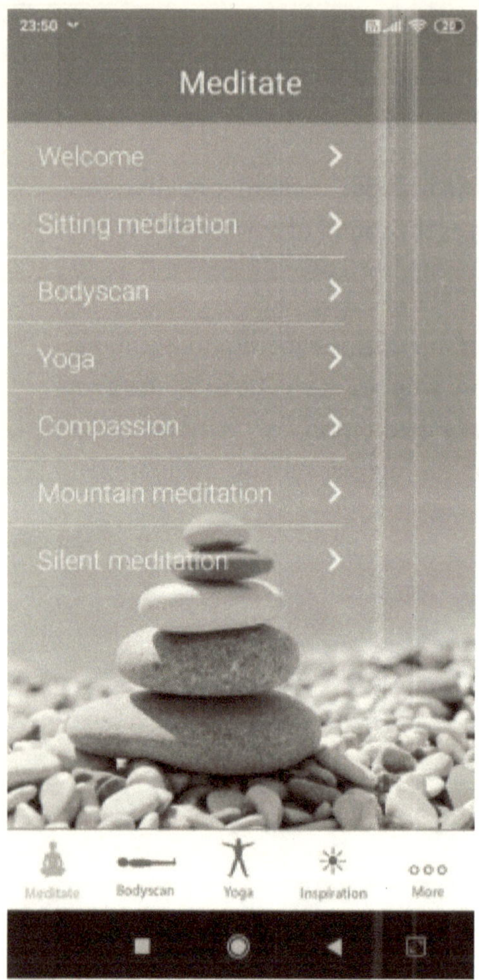

Figure: Screenshot of the Mindfulness App. The app itself is named as "Mindfulness App"

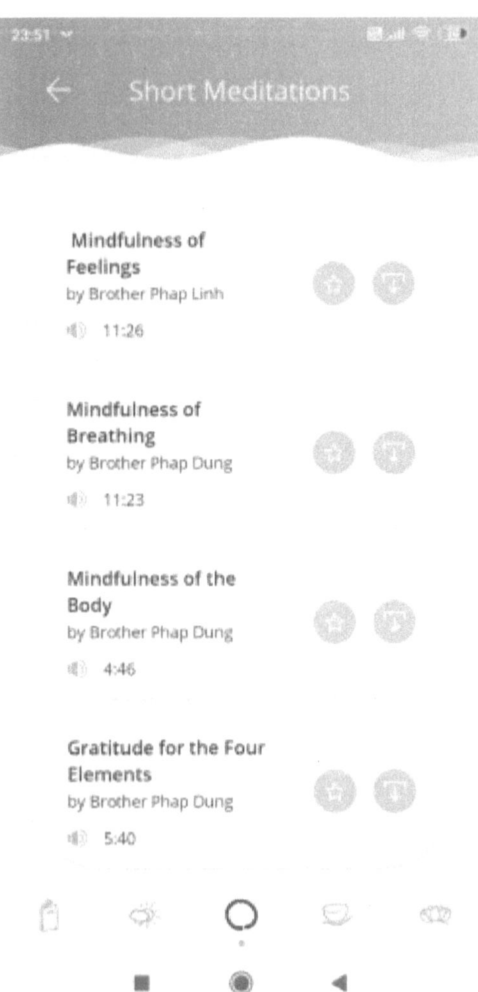

Figure: Screenshot of the Plum Village App showing some of the guided meditations

Figure: Screenshot of the MyLife app.

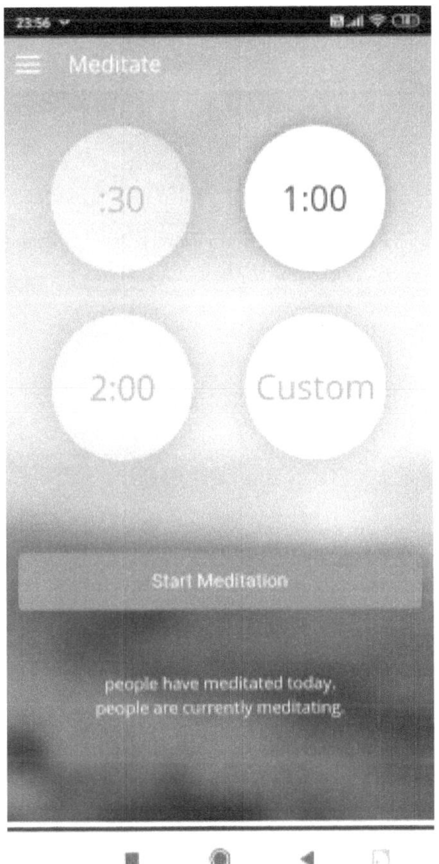

Figure: Screenshot of the Mindfulness app, from UMass Memorial health Care Center for Mindfulness

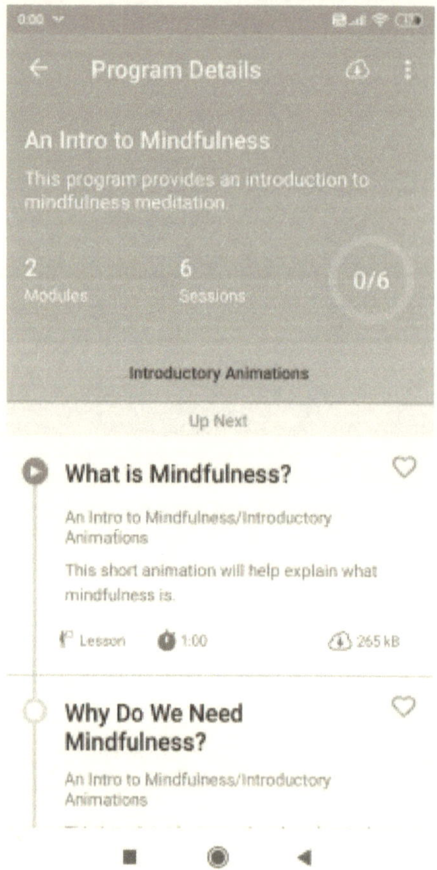

Figure: Screenshot of the Smiling Mind App

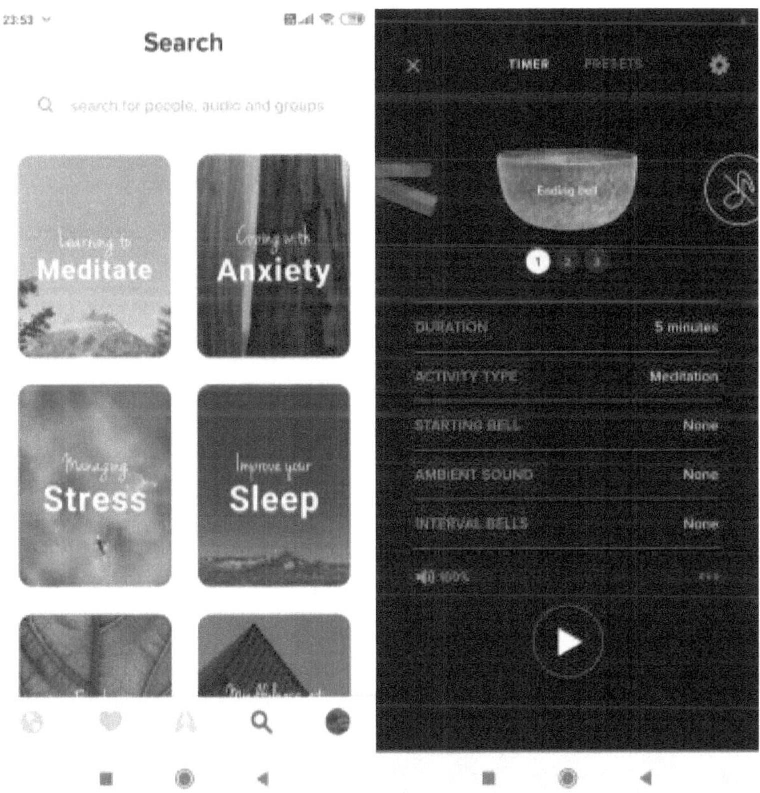

Figure: Screenshots from the Insight Timer App

Figure: Screenshot from the Waking Up app by Sam Harris

Figure: Screenshot from the MyLife App

10.3 Conclusion

In this chapter we have discussed a few apps related to mindfulness meditation, that can be downloaded from the play store or app store on the user's mobile phone. It is worth noting that as of 2024–2025, many leading apps such as Headspace, Calm, and Insight Timer have begun integrating artificial intelligence to personalise session recommendations, track emotional patterns over time, and adapt content to the user's mood and history. A newer generation of AI-powered apps can even generate unique guided meditation sessions on demand based on what the user types in. This rapidly evolving area is discussed further in Chapter 23.

Chapter 11: Browser extensions, PC apps and games related to meditation

In this chapter we discuss a few websites, browser extensions and PC apps that are related to meditation.

11.1 How to get the Chrome extensions

Here focus on the Chrome browser, but similar extensions can be found on other web browsers also.

The chrome extensions can be searched and downloaded from the Chrome Web Store. The website URL is https://chrome.google.com/webstore/category/extensions

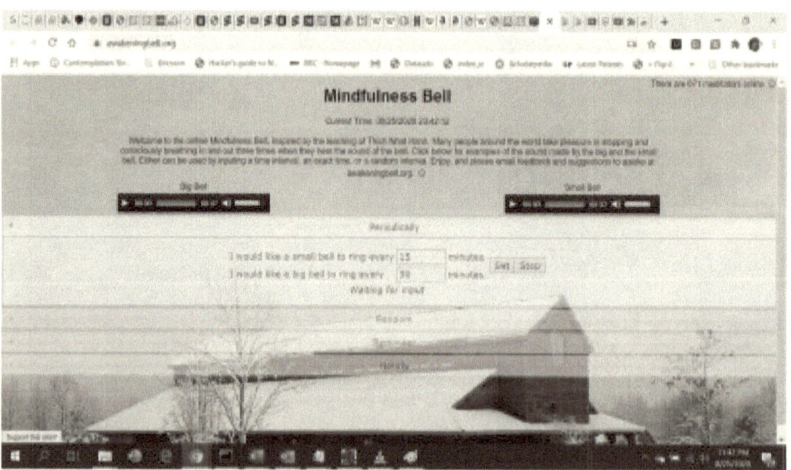

Figure: Screenshot of the Mindfulness Bell website.

11.2 Mindfulness bell website

The URL of the website is https://awakeningbell.org/

This will ring a bell every 15 minutes or as per the settings. The bell reminds to come back to the present moment.

Figure: Bell of Mindfulness Chrome extension.

11.3 Chrome extensions related to meditation

The Chrome extension related to meditation include the following

- The Bell of Mindfulness Chrome extension: This Chrome extension rings a bell every 15 minutes, as a way of reminding you to come back to the present moment. Warning: It is a good idea to to disable this extension when it is time for work meetings, else it can disturb the meeting. The website is https://chrome.google.com/webstore/detail/bell-of-mindfulness/lggmmceliiaoddfnbaccgpfnpoifilic
- Nimbus mind Chrome extension: This is a chrome extension that includes guided meditations. Its website is https://chrome.google.com/webstore/detail/nimbusmind-meditation-rel/accebjobnljiehcaocahignlanfnfkcc

Figure: Screenshot from Coloring Book for me and Mandala. Windows app, downloadable from the Windows store

Figure: Screenshot from Calm Sleep Sounds Windows app, downloadable from the Windows store

Figure: Screenshot form Playne: the Meditation Game

11.4 Windows Apps related to Meditation

Windows apps related to meditation include the following:

◈ Coloring Book for me and Mandala windows app. This can be downloaded from the Windows store. It has various mandalas that one can colour, colouring mandalas is a technique to generate calm.

◈ Calm sleep sounds windows app: This is a windows app that generates relaxing sounds from a variety of sources. It is available for download from the Windows store.

11.5 Games related to meditation

Some games related to meditation include the following:

◈ An example of a mindfulness PC game is Just Sleep (https://store.steampowered.com/app/1093150/ Just_Sleep__Meditate_Focus_Relax/). Just sleep game is available to download from Steam or other gaming platforms.

◇ An example of a game available on Playstation 4 is Flow (https://store.playstation.com/en-us/product/ UP9000-CUSA00144_00-FLOWPLAYSTATION4)

◇ Examples of mindfulness games available on mobile (android/ iOS) include Forest (https://play.google.com/store/apps/ details?id=cc.forestapp&hl=en_US&gl=US) and PAUSE (https://apps.apple.com/us/app/pause-daily-mindfulness/ id991764216).

◇ PLAYNE: The Meditation Game is a Windows game that one can download and install on their Windows Machine via stream. It uses creative visual and gameplay elements to encourage the participants to improve their meditation.

11.6 Conclusion

In this chapter, we have discussed a few meditation related browser apps, PC apps and PC games.

Chapter 12: Wearables and apps based on sounds emitted at certain frequencies

In this chapter, we discuss a few sound based wearable gadgets and apps. These induce a state of meditation by emitting sounds at certain frequencies. The technologies involved include Binaural beats and Pulsed Electromagnetic Field or PEMF.

Figure: Screenshot of the Holosync website

Binaural sound technology uses different sounds from two microphones to give a 3D sound effect. There are a number of apps based on binaural sound, that claim to use binaural beats to produce deep relaxation.

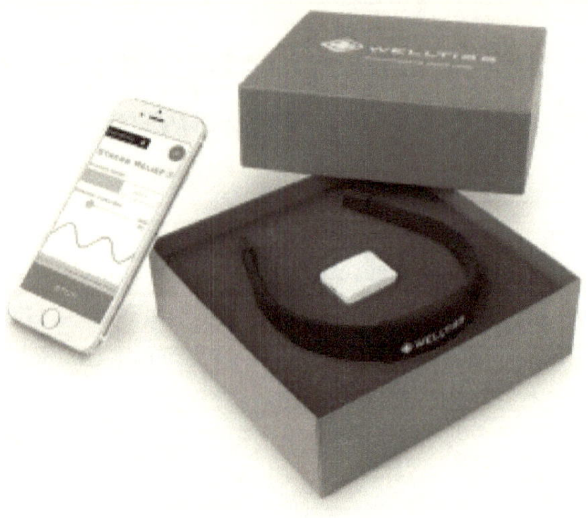

Figure: Weltiss mind headset and app

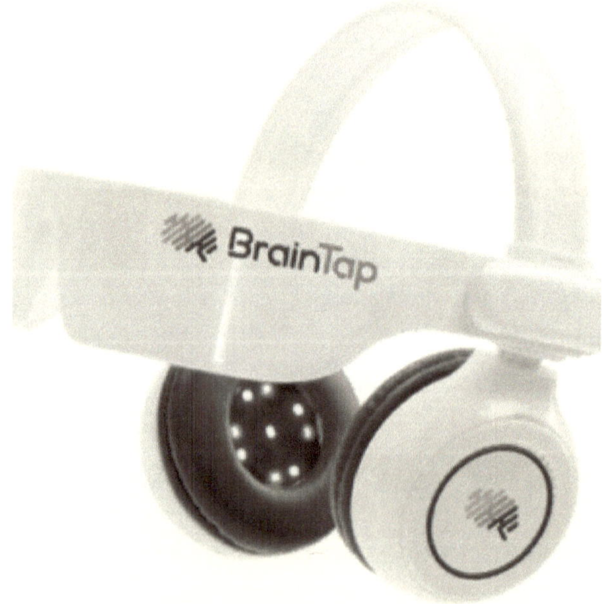

Figure: Braintap headset

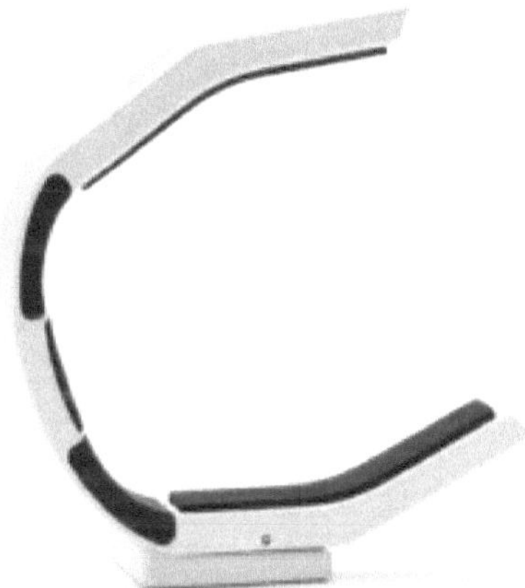

Figure: NeoRythm headband

Some of the wearable gadgets related to sound based meditation include the following:

⬦ Centrepoint's Holosync is one of the technologies that uses binaural sounds to produce a relaxing experience. The website is https://www.holosync.com/

⬦ Weltiss mind device uses a technology called Pulsed Electromagnetic Field or PEMF to perform a similar function i.e. emit sound at certain frequencies to enable the brain to synchronize and go in to deeper relaxed states. This can help for enhancing sleep, meditation, focus etc.

⬦ Braintap is a headset (with an accompanying app) that delivers light and sound pulses to the brain. It uses Binaural beats, along with other technologies such as light frequency therapy, to get the brain into a relaxed state. The website is https://braintap.com/

⬦ NeoRhythm is a wearable headband that uses Pulsed Electromagnetic Field (PEMF) technology for brain stimulation. It claims to improve sleep, meditation, focus and pain management. The website is https://omnipemf.com/

Chapter 13: Gratitude journals and apps to enhance happiness

———

Figure: Screenshot of the Bliss happiness journal app

Research has shown that expressing gratitude and remembering what we are thankful for can go a long way towards enhancing our sense of well-being.

Many apps are available that help one to keep a daily gratitude journal or use other positive psychology tools to enhance happiness.

Some of these apps are as follows:

◇ Reimagining the examen. Website: https://www.ignatianspirituality.com/reimagining-examen-app/

◇ Track your happiness. Website: https://www.trackyourhappiness.org/

◇ Bliss. Website: https://play.google.com/store/apps/details?id=com.bliss.phonegap

◇ Gratitude Journal. Website: https://gratefulness.me/

◇ Happiness Project app. This app contains various techniques to improve the user's happiness, backed by research. The website is https://thehappinessproject.app/

◇ Action for Happiness app: This contains many tips for small actions that the user can take to improve their happiness. The website is https://actionforhappiness.org/app

These happiness journal apps are a great complement to any other meditation apps we may have, to fill in during the day or before going to bed.

Daily reminding ourselves what we are grateful for and going through how the day went and positive experiences we had throughout the day can trick the brain into feeling happier.

Chapter 14: Meditation using Virtual Reality (VR) headsets

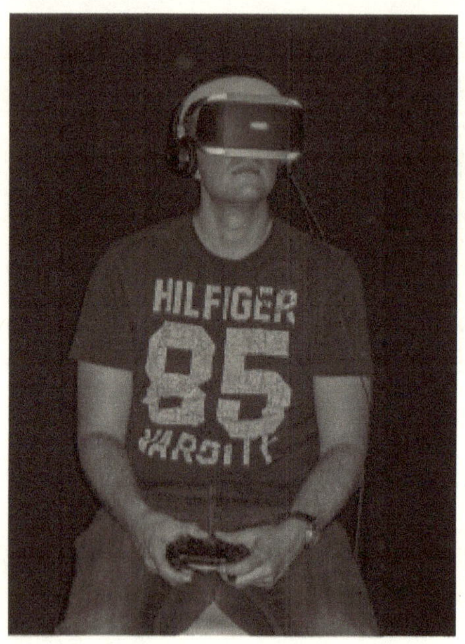

Figure: Using a VR headset By dronepicr — Sony Morpheus Virtual Reality Gamescom 2015 Cologne, CC BY 2.0

There are a growing number of VR-based meditation apps that can be accessed in any VR headset, including Meta Quest (formerly Oculus Rift), PlayStation VR, and Apple Vision Pro.

The VR headset provides an immersive experience that smartphone-based apps generally cannot.

There are a growing number of VR-based meditation apps that can be accessed on any VR headset. Major platforms include Meta Quest (formerly Oculus), PlayStation VR, and Apple Vision Pro (launched in 2024). Popular VR meditation apps include Tripp (https://www.tripp.com/), which offers immersive guided mindfulness sessions and psychedelic visual landscapes;

Guided Meditation VR (available on Meta Quest); and Maloka, a gamified VR wellness app that combines mindfulness with social features. The immersive nature of VR is particularly beneficial for users who struggle to focus during traditional seated meditation, as the visual environment removes real-world distractions entirely. Research suggests that VR-based mindfulness can be especially effective for those dealing with anxiety, chronic pain, or PTSD. A growing number of clinical studies are now exploring VR meditation in therapeutic settings.

Chapter 15: Flotation tanks and float therapy

In this chapter, we discuss floatation tanks, also called sensory deprivation tanks or isolation tanks, which give the subject a sense of meditation by cutting off all sensory stimulation and giving a feeling of weightlessness while the subject is floating in water in the tank.

Figure: Floatation tank

15.1 Introduction to Isolation Tanks or Flotation Tanks

Isolation tanks are not really wearables, but use technology to give a meditation like experience. The person floats in the tank, has a weightless experience and has all the senses shut off, giving a blissful and extraordinarily relaxing experience.

Sensory deprivation has an association with deep states of meditation in some traditions, with Tibetan dark retreats being an important example. Cut off from the senses, the mind can reach states of being that are not easy to reach in the everyday world. Modern day flotation tanks are a continuation of this principle.

The idea of a flotation tank is that we lose all kinds of sensory stimuli, we are floating in salty water in total darkness, total weightlessness and total silence. We are used to being bombarded with stimuli all our lives, mobile phones, endless news, other people, running around etc. So the experience is rather different from what we are used to.

The idea of being in a flotation tank is to cut off all the senses and having no stimulation whatsoever. One just floats in a tank, in complete darkness and quiet. The water is salty and warmed around 32 degrees Celsius, so one can comfortably float and not feel the body or anything touching it. One can close the tank and be in absolute dark or leave it slightly open.

To get the full experience, it is good to do more than one session. The meditation experience becomes progressively deep for many people after the second or third session.

15.2 Where to access flotation tanks

The floatation tanks are available in many cities across the globe, and can be searched easily on google. 1000 Petals in Bangalore India is one such place where one can access this therapy. Their website is http://www.1000petals.in/ The author had a few meditation sessions inside a flotation tank (sensory deprivation tank, isolation tank) at 1000 petals. The flotation tank session was for 60 minutes.

15.3 Setup or preparation before a floatation session

The setup, or preparation, is pretty much common sense and designed to let one get the most of one's experience. Try to get a good night's sleep. Eat a light breakfast or have as less food as possible in the morning of your float session, without any stimulants like tea or coffee. Try to keep a calm mind throughout the day.

When you arrive at the place of the tank at the time of your pre-booked appointment, first you are given a glass of water to drink to keep one hydrated (there is also a water bottle next to the tank in case one needs it). Then you take a quick shower. One has to take off one's clothes and anything else one is wearing such as glasses or a watch. Put earplugs to protect your ears from water.

Turn off the lights in the room and then gently step into the tank. The tank is quite beautiful, big enough to fit your body and shaped a bit like a pearl in an oyster. The managers of the place ensure that the timer is set for exactly an hour and that the tank is warmed up to the appropriate temperature, not too cold and not too hot.

You push the buttons to close the lid of the tank and turn off the blue lights, so you are in complete darkness and nobody to disturb you. When the time is up, the earplugs play gentle music at the end of the hour and the room lights are switched on so that you know when to get up.

Then you have a nice long shower to wash off the salt that might be sticking to your body.

Finally you emerge from the room, rejuvenated, fresh and energized. For the rest of the day, the advice is to not get into too stressful situations so as not to lose the relaxed mind, and maybe later have a short meditation session before going to bed.

15.4 Author's experience of a flotation tank session

For the author, the first session inside a floatation tank felt a bit scary, since we have literally nothing to hold on to, not even the body. The feel of having no support whatsoever and no stimulation is not what we are used to. But after some time, the feeling becomes familiar and one slips into a trance like state or even sleep. one can try to be aware of sensation and thoughts, or breathing, or just let everything go. It's a very unusual experience but soon one hour is over and the session finished.

The author's experience was different from a usual mindfulness meditation session, since here you might tend to lose touch with the breath. It is quite an effort to remain mindful when the environment is so relaxing. But it is not boring at all. The author drifted into a deep sleep like trance.

One is advised to take a shower before and after the session, have little or no food before, including no stimulants like tea, and light food, such as a fruit salad, after.

Overall it was a relaxing and de-stressing experience.

The author then repeated the session after a few weeks.

The second time round, I was determined to really make the most of my time in the flotation tank, and experiment with different kinds of meditations to see which one would work best.

The experience of first closing the lid of the flotation tank was, at least for me, a little scary, so I opted to leave a little bit open. Some of us have a habit of holding on to our ground, even this body, so in a flotation tank when you have to let go of the body completely it can be an unnerving experience. I had a little difficulty in really letting go and not touching at least one of the walls, but eventually managed to float completely. It's a bit strange since even when we sleep, we have to let go, but the ground of the bed is still holding us. Here in the float session, the water is in a way invisible and at the same temperature as the skin, so one loses any feeling of it. Also, the posture of the body is something to be mindful of in the beginning, one has to be straight and relaxed. The hands may float on the sides or on your chest. Moving too much, on the other hand, causes the water to splash and can disturb you. So, it's best to try not to move. I later realized I had forgotten to take off my glasses, but I did not notice it during the whole session!

Bodily movements is one thing, but the mind is of a more difficult nature, since we can't always control our thoughts. So I tried some meditation on specific objects. I began a meditation on the breath, being aware of the in and out breath and the flow of the breath. Taking deep breaths makes the stomach go up and down in rhythm with the breathing. In the total silence one can actually hear ones own breathing quite loudly!

Then I tried some loving kindness meditation, where with each out breath one imagines sending out good vibrations to all beings in the universe. That experience was much better and more powerful than in a normal meditation session. I felt almost floating out of my body. The sense of calm was quite deep. It felt relaxing and I felt a deep feeling of gratitude to have this chance, this experience and the feeling of sharing love and compassion with all beings. I also tried a little bit of openness meditation where one breathes out to the openness of space. Even though I was inside a pod, it didn't feel claustrophobic.

After this mindful session, I drifted off to a kind of deep sleep (which they say is marked by the activation of the theta rhythms of our brain). I only awoke when the hour's time was over and gentle music came though the earphones. An important thing is not to suddenly jump out of the tank, but to take it in slowly and reflect on one's state of mind before stepping out of the tank and into the shower room.

The second time's flotation experience was far more profound than the first time and the author also sensed a feeling of calm that lasted throughout the day. The author would highly recommend anyone who is interested in meditation to have a go at a session inside a flotation tank.

15.5 Difference of a floatation session with a regular meditation session

The experience of a floatation tank session is different from a typical mindfulness meditation session.

In a meditation session (at least the mindfulness one) one typically sits erect on a cushion, is aware of all sensations and in fact, makes an effort to make a mental note of each bodily and thought stimuli (such as breathing, itches, pains, thoughts) without getting too deeply into any of them.

In a floatation session, one doesn't have to do anything consciously, although one can choose to if he or she wishes. The setup is such that deep relaxation and meditative states naturally happen. We humans have a natural affinity with water, floating on warm water gives an impression of floating in space. It is a bit like being in a womb.

15.6 Conclusion

In this chapter, we have reviewed floatation tanks as a tool for meditation and described the author's subjective experience of a floatation tank session.

Chapter 16: Lucia Light Therapy

In this chapter, we survey a light therapy machine called Lucia Light Therapy.

16.1 How does light therapy work

Light therapy works in the following way: The person sits in a comfortable posture, closes the eyes, then light patterns are shown on the closed eyes by a specialized machine. The light patterns, along with synchronized music, work to activate the energy of the chakras at the position of the 'third eye' on one's forehead, or the pineal gland. They enable the subject to go into a meditation 'theta' deep state. The light therapy session typically lasts for around 30 minutes.

16.2 The author's experience with Lucia Light Therapy

The author went for a light therapy session at Bangalore's 1000 petals in India.

After sitting in a comfortable position, the Lucia Light Therapy machine was started which showed light on the subject's eyes. The light patterns vary from slowly changing bright and dim light along with relaxing music, with which one has to synchronize the breathing.

Next come faster lights in different patterns, where one gets a feeling of floating or moving with the light. Depending upon ones background, one might hallucinate different shapes and figures.

The author's feeling was quite strange. At first it was just lots of light shining on your forehead. Then at some point, the attention moves away from the body feelings and towards the space created by the light patterns. One feels at one with the light, as if we have an ethereal body and are floating upwards, dancing with the lights. It's almost as if the body doesn't exist and one is expanding consciousness to the world. The feeling is of immense joy and of being at one with everything. Who would have thought a simple light session could work such wonders?

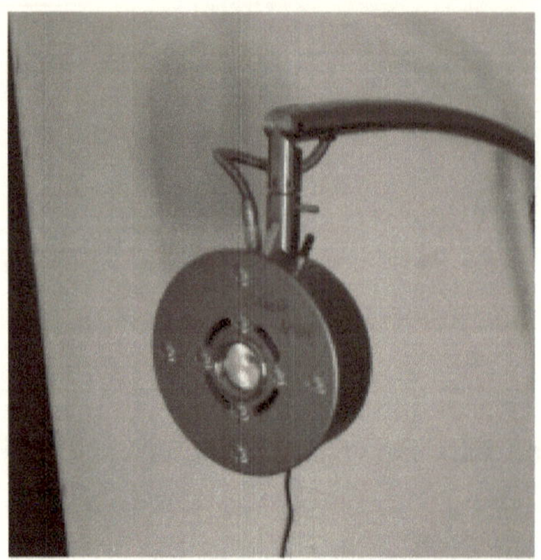

Figure: Lucia light therapy apparatus

16.3 Conclusion

In this chapter, we discussed the Lucia Light Therapy machine, which shines varying patterns of light on the subject's eye to activate the pineal gland and induce a very relaxing experience of expanded consciousness.

Chapter 17: Research on mindfulness apps and wearable gadgets for stress reduction

In this chapter, we discuss and review a few papers that study the effect of mindfulness apps and wearables on stress levels and overall well-being of users.

17.1 Research on effectiveness of mindfulness apps in stress reduction

In an 8-weeks workplace study on effects on the **Headspace** mindfulness app on 238 office users in UK (Bostock et al., 2019), the app users showed significant and sustained improvement in well-being.

In a study of university students using the **Calm app** (Huberty et al., 2019), app users reported a significant improvement in reducing stress levels. Huberty et al. (2021) also found that Calm app subscribers had better sleep quality. Another study of Calm meditation app users during the Covid 19 pandemic (Cloonan et al., 2023), participants showed reduced levels of worrying.

A meta-analysis of papers related to mindfulness apps (Gal et al., 2021) found reduced stress and enhanced well-being for app users.

Truhlar et al. (2022) explored the effect of the meditation app called **Ten Percent Happier** on pharmacy students and found that regular use of the app resulted in improved mindfulness, well-being and resilience.

Walsh et al. (2019) experimented with a mindfulness app called **Wildflowers** with 41 undergraduate university students and found it resulted in improved mood, stress reduction and attention control among the students.

17.2 Research on wearable devices for well-being and stress reduction

Lee et al. (2024) experimented on university community participants in Korea with a EEG based Neurofeedback device called **MAVE**, with the participants being asked to do meditation while their EEG was measured, and found that the participants had improvements in stress, depression and anxiety.

Chianella et al. (2021) studied the effectiveness of multimodal **smartwatch** wearables for stress tracking and found that overall they were useful, with suggestions on how to make them more useful.

There are a number of studies on stress and wellness using the **MUSE** meditation headband. Millstine et al. (2019) experimented with the wearable MUSE meditation headband on 30 female users with breast cancer, and found that use of the headband helped in reducing fatigue and enhancing functional well-being among the study users. Ghosh et al. (2023) experimented with the MUSE wearable with guided meditation on 40 health care professionals for 90 days during Covid-19 pandemic and found reduced stress and improved resilience and quality of life. Balconi et al. (2019) experimented with mindfulness practice combined with wearable devices with Neurofeedback including **Lowdown Focus** glasses (for eye tracking) and MUSE headband on 55 young adults and found positive results in stress reduction.

17.3 Conclusion

There are a number of available studies on stress reduction using mindfulness apps such as Calm and headspace and wearables such as MUSE meditation headband. While their exact recommendations and findings vary, overall they report positive results on stress reduction and wellness related parameters in users of these apps and wearable devices. Therefore, such consumer apps and wearables, which are readily available in the market, may be useful for users to manage their stress in daily life.

References

Balconi, M., Fronda, G., & Crivelli, D. (2019). Effects of technology-mediated mindfulness practice on stress: psychophysiological and self-report measures. Stress, 22(2), 200–209.

Bostock, S., Crosswell, A. D., Prather, A. A., & Steptoe, A. (2019). Mindfulness on-the-go: Effects of a mindfulness meditation app on work stress and well-being. Journal of occupational health psychology, 24(1), 127.

Chianella, R., Mandolfo, M., Lolatto, R., & Pillan, M. (2021, July). Designing for self-awareness: evidence-based explorations of multimodal stress-tracking wearables. In International Conference on Human-Computer Interaction (pp. 357–371). Cham: Springer International Publishing.

Cloonan, S., Fowers, R., Huberty, J., & Stecher, C. (2023). Meditation App Habits and Mental Health: A Longitudinal Study of Meditation App Users During the COVID-19 Pandemic. Mindfulness, 14(9), 2276–2286.

Gál, É., Ştefan, S., & Cristea, I. A. (2021). The efficacy of mindfulness meditation apps in enhancing users' well-being and mental health related outcomes: a meta-analysis of randomized controlled trials. Journal of Affective Disorders, 279, 131–142.

Ghosh, K., Nanda, S., Hurt, R. T., Schroeder, D. R., West, C. P., Fischer, K. M., ... & Croghan, I. T. (2023). Mindfulness using a wearable brain sensing device for health care professionals during a pandemic: A pilot program. Journal of Primary Care & Community Health, 14, 21501319231162308.

Huberty, J., Green, J., Glissmann, C., Larkey, L., Puzia, M., & Lee, C. (2019). Efficacy of the mindfulness meditation mobile app "calm" to reduce stress among college students: Randomized controlled trial. JMIR mHealth and uHealth, 7(6), e14273.

Huberty, J., Puzia, M. E., Larkey, L., Vranceanu, A. M., & Irwin, M. R. (2021). Can a meditation app help my sleep? A cross-sectional survey of Calm users. PLoS One, 16(10), e0257518.

Lee, E., Hong, J. K., Choi, H., & Yoon, I. Y. (2024). Modest Effects of Neurofeedback-Assisted Meditation Using a Wearable Device on Stress Reduction: A Randomized, Double-Blind, and Controlled Study. Journal of Korean Medical Science, 39(9).

Millstine, D. M., Bhagra, A., Jenkins, S. M., Croghan, I. T., Stan, D. L., Boughey, J. C., ... & Pruthi, S. (2019). Use of a wearable EEG headband as a meditation device for women with newly diagnosed breast cancer: a randomized controlled trial. Integrative Cancer Therapies, 18, 1534735419878770.

Truhlar, L. M., Durand, C., Cooper, M. R., & Goldsmith, C. A. W. (2022). Exploring the effects of a smartphone-based meditation app on stress, mindfulness, well-being, and resilience in pharmacy students. American Journal of Health-System Pharmacy, 79(23), 2159–2165.

Walsh, K. M., Saab, B. J., & Farb, N. A. (2019). Effects of a mindfulness meditation app on subjective well-being: active randomized controlled trial and experience sampling study. JMIR mental health, 6(1), e10844.

Chapter 18: Mindful Productivity and Tech Tools for Focus

In this chapter, we discuss how certain technology tools and apps can be used to enhance mindful productivity and help reduce distractions during work. For those who work long hours on the computer or mobile phone, especially in demanding fields like IT or digital marketing, this chapter provides practical suggestions for using technology to stay focused, reduce stress, and increase clarity of mind throughout the day.

Just like mindfulness meditation helps bring awareness to our present moment, certain apps and digital tools can act as external supports or reminders for maintaining focus and calm during our workday. When used properly, they can help us work in a more conscious, relaxed and effective manner.

18.1 Problems in modern work environments

For many of us, work involves long hours sitting in front of a screen. Some common problems people face include:

◇ Constant distractions due to notifications, messages and emails

◇ Mental fatigue from multitasking and context switching

◇ Difficulty in prioritizing tasks

◇ Forgetting to take regular breaks or hydrate

◇ Shallow breathing and poor posture

These can all contribute to stress, anxiety and burnout over time. A few simple tech tools and changes in habits can make a big difference.

18.2 Mindful productivity tools

Here are some categories of tech tools and apps that can help improve productivity in a mindful and balanced way.

a. Pomodoro timers and focus apps

Pomodoro technique is a simple method that breaks work into 25-minute focused sessions followed by 5-minute breaks.

◈ Focus To-Do (https://www.focustodo.cn/) combines Pomodoro with task management.

◈ Forest (https://www.forestapp.cc/) is a mobile app that grows a tree when you stay focused.

◈ Tide (https://tide.fm/en_US/) combines timer with relaxing natural sounds.

These help prevent burnout and train the mind to focus on one task at a time.

b. Distraction blocker apps

◈ StayFocusd (Chrome Extension): Blocks time-wasting websites during work hours.

◈ Freedom (https://freedom.to/): Blocks internet, apps or websites across devices.

◈ Cold Turkey (https://getcoldturkey.com/): Useful for scheduled deep work sessions.

These help reduce the constant urge to check social media or news.

c. Mindful scheduling and to-do lists

These include the following:

◈ Notion (https://www.notion.so/): Combines note-taking, task lists, databases and calendars.

◈ Todoist (https://todoist.com/): A simple and effective task manager.

◈ Sunsama (https://sunsama.com/): Encourages daily planning and intentional work.

These apps help you review your priorities and avoid overwhelm.

d. Mindful email and communication tools

Some examples of such tools are as follows:

◈ Boomerang for Gmail: Lets you schedule emails and reminders.

◈ Slack Do Not Disturb mode: Avoids interruptions during focused work.

◈ Emailga.me: Turns your inbox into a game to clear mails mindfully.

18.3 Smart reminders for mindfulness

We can set periodic reminders for taking mindful breaks, stretching or checking posture.

◈ Use Google Calendar to block focus time.

◈ Use Stretchly (https://hovancik.net/stretchly/) or Workrave for break reminders.

◈ Set reminders on your smartwatch or phone for deep breaths or gratitude.

◈ Create a desktop wallpaper with calming quotes or reminders.

These act like modern-day bells of mindfulness.

18.4 Simple workspace changes for mindful tech use

◇ Keep a glass of water nearby and sip mindfully.

◇ Use blue light filters like f.lux or Night Light mode in evening hours.

◇ Keep your phone face down and turn off non-essential notifications.

◇ Use apps in grayscale mode to reduce compulsive checking.

◇ Add plants or calming visuals in your workspace.

18.5 Mindful shutdown ritual at end of day

At the end of the workday, it helps to:

◇ Review your day mindfully: What went well, what to improve

◇ Shut down your laptop intentionally and slowly

◇ Avoid tech gadgets for 30–60 minutes before sleep

◇ Do a short 5-minute breathing or gratitude meditation

18.6 Conclusion

Mindful productivity means being fully present and conscious while doing our work. It involves managing technology instead of being controlled by it. With a few changes in how we use digital tools, we can work with greater clarity, purpose and well-being.

Chapter 19: Digital Minimalism for Meditators

In this chapter, we explore the idea of digital minimalism—how simplifying our digital lives can help us reclaim our attention and deepen our meditation practice. In today's world of constant connectivity, we often find ourselves overstimulated, distracted, and mentally scattered. Digital minimalism is the conscious practice of reducing unnecessary digital clutter so that we can be more mindful, present and peaceful throughout the day.

Digital minimalism does not mean giving up technology. It means using it with awareness, intention, and discipline, so that it serves our values rather than distracting from them.

19.1 Signs that you may need digital minimalism

Some signs that your digital life may be negatively affecting your mindfulness include:

◈ Checking the phone first thing after waking up

◈ Spending long hours scrolling through social media

◈ Feeling anxious when away from the phone

◈ Multitasking between apps, tabs and notifications

◈ Difficulty sitting still or focusing without digital input

These habits fragment attention and increase stress. They also make it harder to enter a calm meditative state.

19.2 Principles of digital minimalism

Here are some principles that can help guide a mindful use of technology:

◈ **Clarity before tools**: Ask yourself what you truly value (e.g., focus, creativity, compassion) before choosing which apps or gadgets to use.

◈ **Intentionality**: Use digital tools for specific purposes and then log off.

◈ **Timeboxing**: Allocate specific time windows for email, news, and social media.

◈ **Low information diet**: Choose a few reliable sources of information, and avoid endless scrolling.

◈ **Solitude matters**: Protect time in your day where you are alone with your thoughts.

19.3 Practical steps to simplify your digital life

These small actions can help create more peace and presence in your day:

◈ Uninstall unnecessary apps and turn off non-essential notifications.

◈ Keep only a few core meditation or wellness apps—don't overload.

◈ Use grayscale mode on your phone to reduce the visual stimulation.

◈ Move distracting apps off the home screen or uninstall them.

◈ Create tech-free spaces or hours in your home (e.g., no phone in bedroom).

◈ Use email and messaging apps only during certain hours of the day.

◈ Practice one-screen focus: Close all extra tabs or windows while working.

19.4 The digital sabbath

Inspired by traditional Sabbath practices, many digital minimalists now take one day a week (often Sunday) to completely unplug from screens. This digital rest day helps reset attention, reconnect with loved ones, and ground yourself in the present.

Even shorter sabbaticals—such as no phone for the first hour in the morning and the last hour at night—can have big benefits.

19.5 Using tech mindfully without giving it up

You do not have to give up technology to be mindful. Instead:

◈ Use focus timers to train single-tasking.

◈ Replace compulsive app use with a short breathing break.

◈ Set a wallpaper or lock screen quote that reminds you of your values.

◈ Combine movement with mindfulness—listen to walking meditations instead of browsing.

◈ Use your smartwatch or smart ring to check stress, not messages.

19.6 How digital minimalism supports meditation

Digital minimalism helps your meditation by:

◈ Creating a calm and spacious mind with fewer distractions

◈ Helping you build the habit of non-reactivity (e.g., to notifications)

◈ Making it easier to stick to daily meditation routines

◈ Allowing deeper insight during sessions due to lower input overload

As the mind becomes less cluttered, it becomes easier to observe it during meditation.

19.7 Conclusion

Digital minimalism is not about rejecting technology, but about refining your relationship with it. By reducing the digital noise around us, we can hear the quiet voice within. This practice creates space in our day—and in our mind—for true mindfulness to flourish.

Chapter 20: Smart Home Meditation Integration

In this chapter, we explore how to set up a mindful and calming meditation space using smart home technologies like Alexa, Google Nest, Philips Hue smart lights, and automation tools such as IFTTT. These technologies, when used wisely, can help create an environment that supports regular meditation practice, reduces distractions, and fosters inner calm.

Smart homes are no longer just about convenience—they can also be tools for well-being. With a few simple setups, our home environment can become a subtle reminder to pause, breathe, and reconnect with the present moment.

20.1 Smart speakers as meditation assistants

Smart speakers like **Amazon Alexa** or **Google Nest** can be used to:

◈ Play guided meditations on command

◈ Set daily meditation reminders

◈ Play relaxing nature sounds (e.g., ocean waves, rain, forest sounds)

◈ Control lighting and ambiance with voice commands

◈ Enable focus timers using voice (e.g., "Alexa, start 15-minute meditation timer")

How to set up:

◈ Enable meditation skills or apps like **Headspace**, **Calm**, or **Meditation Timer** via the Alexa or Google Home app.

◈ Use routines to start your session (e.g., saying "Alexa, start my meditation" could turn off lights, play a gong, and start a 10-minute guided session).

20.2 Using smart lights for ambiance

Smart bulbs like **Philips Hue**, **Wyze Bulbs**, or **LIFX** allow you to:

◈ Set warm, soft lighting for evening meditations

◈ Use cooler lights for morning alertness

◈ Slowly dim or brighten to simulate sunrise or sunset

◈ Match color tones with the type of meditation (e.g., blue for calm, orange for energy)

Tips:

◈ Use a preset called "Relax" or create a custom one with dimmed yellow light.

◈ Avoid harsh white or blue light late at night as it disrupts melatonin.

◈ Link smart lights with meditation routines using IFTTT or Alexa routines.

20.3 Automating mindfulness with IFTTT

IFTTT (If This Then That) is a powerful tool that connects various devices and apps to automate tasks.

Examples of useful IFTTT automations:

◈ If the clock hits 7 AM, **then** play a morning chant + turn on warm lights.

◈ If you say "Alexa, meditation time," **then** turn off phone notifications (via Android integration) + dim the lights.

◈ If it's sunset, **then** play ambient sounds from a playlist.

◈ If stress levels rise (using smart ring or watch), **then** start a short breathing exercise on Google Nest.

To use IFTTT:

◈ Visit https://ifttt.com[1] and connect your smart devices.

◈ Browse existing applets or create your own custom automations.

20.4 Creating a tech-enhanced meditation corner

Here's how you can build a simple, smart meditation nook:

◈ **Smart speaker** (for voice commands and audio)

◈ **Smart lights** (for ambiance)

◈ **Phone dock** or device tray (to keep gadgets out of reach but connected)

◈ **Optional: Aroma diffuser** connected to a smart plug to turn on automatically

◈ **Cushion, mat or chair** for physical comfort

Set up the space to require minimal interaction. Let the environment support your intention.

20.5 Ideas for daily smart meditation routines

Morning:

---

1. https://ifttt.com/

◈ 6:30 AM: Smart light slowly brightens

◈ 6:35 AM: Nature sounds start playing on Alexa

◈ 6:40 AM: Guided meditation plays for 10 minutes

Evening:

◈ 9:00 PM: Lights dim to warm amber

◈ 9:05 PM: Play calm flute music or chanting

◈ 9:30 PM: Reminder for gratitude journaling

These routines can help make mindfulness an easy and natural part of your day.

20.6 Conclusion

A smart home meditation setup isn't about complexity. It's about reducing friction. When your space automatically supports calm and stillness, it becomes easier to stay consistent with your meditation practice. By combining the power of smart devices with mindful intention, we can create environments that gently lead us inward.

In the following chapters, we continue exploring other ways that technology can enhance—not distract from—our journey toward peace and awareness.

Chapter 21: Traditional Meditation Frameworks and How Gadgets Compare

In this chapter, we explore some traditional meditation systems—such as the Buddhist Jhana stages, the Yogic path from Pratyahara to Dhyana, and the Dzogchen and Zen approaches to meditation—and compare them with the kind of feedback offered by modern meditation gadgets like HRV monitors, EEG headsets, and smart wearables.

While gadgets can provide helpful cues and motivation for beginners, it is important to remember that the core of meditation practice lies in awareness, presence, and letting go—not in chasing numbers or external validation. Understanding traditional frameworks can help ensure that technology becomes a support, not a distraction, on the meditative path.

21.1 Buddhist Jhana Stages and Meditation Gadgets

The Jhanas are a set of meditative absorptions described in Theravada Buddhism. These stages are marked by increasing stillness, focus, and joy.

Key stages:

- **First Jhana**: Applied and sustained attention, joy, pleasure

- **Second Jhana**: Deeper joy and one-pointedness

- **Third Jhana**: Equanimity and bodily ease

- **Fourth Jhana**: Pure equanimity and mindfulness

How gadgets relate:

- **HRV and breath monitors** may show increasing calm as one enters deeper Jhana-like states.

◈ **EEG devices** (e.g., Muse, Neurosky) may reflect increased alpha or theta brainwave activity, associated with relaxation and one-pointedness.

Limits:

These devices can indicate external signs of calm, but they cannot detect the internal qualities of joy, rapture, or insight that define the Jhanas.

21.2 Yogic Stages: From Pratyahara to Dhyana

In the Yogic tradition (as described in Patanjali's Yoga Sutras), the inner journey involves eight limbs. Of these, three are inward-facing and related to meditation:

◈ **Pratyahara**: Withdrawal of the senses

◈ **Dharana**: Concentration on a single object

◈ **Dhyana**: Effortless meditation or absorption

How gadgets relate:

◈ Gadgets may assist with **Dharana**, helping develop sustained attention through feedback (e.g., HRV coherence or EEG meditation scores).

◈ However, **Pratyahara**—withdrawing from sensory distractions—and **Dhyana**—effortless immersion—cannot be produced by external tools alone.

Yogic caution:

Reliance on gadgets may actually stimulate the senses more, pulling attention outward. The goal in Yoga is to turn attention inward and become the observer.

21.3 Dzogchen and Zen Approaches

Both Dzogchen (Tibetan Buddhism) and Zen emphasize the direct experience of awareness, without conceptual elaboration.

◈ **Dzogchen** points to the natural state of mind: open, empty, luminous.

◈ **Zen** focuses on "just sitting" (zazen), observing thoughts without clinging.

View on gadgets:

◈ These traditions often avoid reliance on props, words, or techniques.

◈ They emphasize the direct recognition of mind as it is—something no metric can capture.

A Dzogchen or Zen master might say: "The moment you check your score, you've already left the meditation."

21.4 How to Use Meditation Gadgets Mindfully

While these traditions caution against overuse of tools, gadgets can be skillful means if used with wisdom.

Guidelines:

◈ **Use as a mirror, not a measurement**: Treat data as feedback, not judgment.

◈ **Let go after the session**: Avoid reviewing scores obsessively. Trust your felt experience.

◈ **Start with gadgets, then let them go**: Use tools to build the habit. Gradually shift toward inner guidance.

◈ **Avoid competition**: Meditation is not a sport. There are no medals for lowest heart rate.

◈ **Combine with journaling or reflection**: After using a device, reflect on how the session felt, not just what the numbers say.

21.5 Integration of Tech and Tradition

A balanced path may look like:

◈ Morning: Guided meditation with Muse or HRV tracker

◈ Evening: Silent sitting without tech, focused on awareness

◈ Weekly: Reflection on progress using both personal journal and gadget feedback

◈ Occasional: Retreat or device-free day for deeper presence

21.6 Conclusion

Traditional meditation frameworks offer depth and clarity on the path toward inner peace and awakening. Modern gadgets can be helpful companions, especially in the early stages, but they are not substitutes for real insight or transformation. By learning from both ancient wisdom and modern technology, we can walk the path with both precision and heart.

Chapter 22: Suggested Daily Routines Using Tech for Mindfulness

In this chapter, we provide sample daily routines that integrate mindfulness meditation with modern tech tools and gadgets. These routines are suggestions to help bring structure and consistency to your practice throughout the day—whether you're a beginner looking to get started, or an experienced practitioner seeking to deepen your habits with the support of wearable or digital aids.

The day can be naturally divided into three parts: morning, midday, and evening. Each phase has different energy and opportunities to bring awareness into your life.

22.1 Morning Routine: Awakening Mindfully

Goal: Set a calm and clear tone for the day ahead.

Tools:

- **Dhyana Ring** or **Unyte IOM2**

- **Guided Meditation App** (e.g., Insight Timer, Calm, Headspace)

- **Smart Lights** or **Smart Speaker** (for setting ambiance)

Routine Example:

- Wake up and hydrate.

- Sit comfortably, wear the Dhyana Ring.

- Start a 10-minute guided meditation from your chosen app.

- Let the ring provide biofeedback on your HRV and focus.

◇ Optional: Use Alexa or smart light preset to create a gentle lighting environment.

◇ Reflect on a simple intention or gratitude before beginning your workday.

22.2 Midday Routine: Reset and Recalibrate

Goal: Reduce stress, improve posture and focus.

Tools:

◇ **Pomodoro Timer App** (e.g., Focus To-Do, Forest)

◇ **Posture Reminder** (e.g., Upright Go or smart band)

◇ **Breathing Coach App** (e.g., Breathe+, Prana Breath)

Routine Example:

◇ After 2–3 hours of work, take a tech-supported mindful break.

◇ Use a Pomodoro app to do 25 minutes of focused work.

◇ Follow it with 5 minutes of mindful breathing (guided by an app).

◇ Do a quick posture scan with feedback from a wearable or app.

◇ Stretch or take a mindful walk, without screens.

This mini reset can dramatically boost afternoon productivity and reduce fatigue.

22.3 Evening Routine: Unwind and Reflect

Goal: Wind down, relax deeply, and sleep better.

Tools:

◇ **Floatation Tank** (if accessible)

◈ **Binaural Beats or Sound App** (e.g., Brain.fm, Holosync)

◈ **Smart Light** (set to warm amber tones)

◈ **Gratitude Journal App** (e.g., Bliss, Day One)

Routine Example:

◈ If available, schedule a 45–60 min float tank session to deeply relax body and mind.

◈ At home, create a dim environment using smart lighting.

◈ Play 20 minutes of binaural beats or ambient meditation music.

◈ Sit in silent meditation or do a guided body scan.

◈ Reflect on the day and write 3 things you're grateful for in a journaling app.

◈ Put your phone away 30 minutes before bed.

22.4 Weekly Tips:

◈ Choose one day per week as a "tech-light" or "device-free" mindfulness day.

◈ Join a live Zoom meditation group or community once a week for support.

◈ Review your gadget data only once per week to avoid overanalysing daily metrics.

22.5 Conclusion:

Routines supported by technology can help automate mindfulness into your day—but the most important element is your intention. Allow these tools to serve your awareness, not replace it. Use them like training wheels, eventually learning to ride the wave of awareness unaided, with peace and presence throughout your day.

Chapter 23: Next-Generation Gadgets and the Future of Mindful Tech

Technology for mindfulness continues to evolve rapidly. In the last few years, several innovative devices have emerged that help people build meditation routines or deepen their self-awareness. This chapter introduces some of the most important new gadgets (2023–2025) designed for mindfulness and meditation. Each device is practical and non-invasive, aligning with a calm and evidence-informed approach rather than gimmicks. We focus on wearables and neurotechnology – from brain-sensing headbands to smart rings – and compare them with earlier gadgets discussed in the book.

23.1 Muse S "Athena" – Dual Sensor Brain-Sensing Headband

Name: Muse S (Athena)

Function: EEG and fNIRS based headband for meditation and cognitive training. It provides real-time neurofeedback to improve focus, endurance, and relaxation. Athena is the first consumer wearable to combine electroencephalography (EEG) (brainwave tracking) with functional near-infrared spectroscopy (fNIRS) (brain blood oxygenation measurement) . This dual-sensor setup gives a richer picture of the user's mental state, both instant brain activity and the effort the brain is exerting. During meditation sessions or exercises in the Muse app, Athena can guide the user with biofeedback – for example, an interactive exercise has you keep a virtual owl flying by sustaining focus.

Release Date: Announced in early 2025 (Toronto, March 2025). Muse Athena represents the next generation after the Muse 2 and Muse S headbands.

Official Product Page: choosemuse.com – Muse S (Athena)

Comparison: Compared to earlier Muse models (discussed previously in this book), Athena adds a new layer of insight. The original Muse and Muse 2 used

EEG to give real-time feedback on mental calm or attention. Athena builds on that by also tracking frontal cortex blood flow, which helps gauge cognitive effort and stress levels more directly. This means it can be used not only for traditional eyes-closed meditation, but also for "eyes-open" focus training and even sleep monitoring. In tone and purpose it remains similar to the Muse devices readers know – a gentle coach for the mind – but with more advanced sensors enabling features like measuring mental endurance and guiding recovery after mental strain.

23.2 FocusCalm Headband – Affordable EEG Neurofeedback Trainer

Name: FocusCalm EEG Headband

Function: An EEG-based brain-training headband that uses neurofeedback games and guided meditations to cultivate a calmer, more focused mind. The FocusCalm device sits lightly on the forehead and connects to a smartphone app. As you meditate or play its simple brain-training games, it measures your brain's electrical activity and gives you a "FocusCalm score" in real time. The goal is to learn to lower stress and enter a focused-yet-relaxed state more easily, using the feedback as a guide.

Release Date: First released in 2021 (gaining broader availability by 2022). It was developed by BrainCo, a startup out of the Harvard Innovation Labs.

Official Product Page: focuscalm.com

Comparison: FocusCalm offers a more budget-friendly alternative to devices like Muse. Priced around $249 (with an optional app subscription), it lowers the entry barrier for EEG neurofeedback. FocusCalm takes a different approach than audio feedback in devices like Muse, often involving simple games and visual exercises to engage the user. This makes it feel a bit like a mobile app experience combined with a headband, whereas Muse leans more on traditional meditation with sound feedback.

23.3 Oura Ring Gen3 – Smart Ring for Mindful Living

Name: Oura Ring (Generation 3) – Horizon & Heritage models

Function: A smart ring that tracks key health metrics (heart rate, heart rate variability, sleep stages, body temperature, etc.) to provide insight into your recovery, stress, and readiness each day. While the Oura Ring is not a meditation device per se, it supports mindfulness by helping users understand their body's patterns and by offering built-in sessions for breathing and meditation. The Gen3 Oura ring introduced daytime stress monitoring and improved accuracy over previous versions. For example, it can detect when your body shows signs of stress during the day and prompt you with a gentle reminder or a suggestion to take a breathing break. The Oura app also includes a library of guided meditations and breathing exercises, and the ring's bio-data can show how these practices affect your physiology (like raising your HRV or calming your heart rate).

Release Date: Generation 3 was released in late 2021, with the refined "Horizon" design (a perfectly round ring with no flat edges) launching in late 2022. Throughout 2023, software updates added features like daytime "Stress Resilience" scores and improved algorithms.

Official Product Page: ouraring.com (Oura Ring Gen3)

Comparison: Earlier in the book we explored smart rings. The Oura Gen3 stands out as the leading smart ring in recent years. It goes beyond the nightly sleep tracking of Gen2 by adding all-day heart rate and stress tracking, making it more comparable to high-end smartwatches in capability. Compared to wearing a smartwatch or chest strap for heart rate variability, many users find a ring less obtrusive. In terms of mindfulness support, the Gen3's introduction of daytime wellness insights and an integrated meditation library sets it apart from earlier rings that might only record data. It provides an intuitive readiness score each morning to gauge if you should take it easy or push yourself – indirectly encouraging self-awareness and balance, much like having a digital coach.

23.4 Apollo Neuro – Wearable Vibration for Stress Relief

Name: Apollo Neuro

Function: A wearable device (worn on the wrist or ankle) that uses gentle vibrations to improve resilience to stress and aid relaxation. Apollo Neuro doesn't record your biometrics; instead, it actively stimulates your sense of touch. The device emits subtle vibrating waves at frequencies tuned to signal safety and calm to the body. According to its developers, these vibrations help "rebalance" your nervous system out of fight-or-flight mode . In practice, you can run different programs (via the Apollo smartphone app) – for example, a 15-minute "Relax and Unwind" session where the band buzzes in a soothing pattern. Users often wear Apollo during the day to stay calm under pressure or at night to help wind down for sleep. Over time, consistent use aims to improve your heart rate variability (HRV) and stress recovery, a sign of a more resilient nervous system.

Release Date: Apollo Neuro was first released in 2020. It gained wider attention through 2021–2023 as studies and user reports emerged. (It was developed by a neuroscientist and psychiatrist team and launched via crowdfunding.)

Official Product Page: apolloneuro.com

Comparison: The Apollo Neuro represents a new category of mindfulness tech that we only touched on previously – wearable neuromodulation. Earlier in the book, we looked at devices that measure your stress (like heart rate monitors) or guide you via biofeedback. Apollo instead actively intervenes with sense-based stimulation. It could be compared to the tactile "TouchPoints" devices (small vibrating discs for each hand) or even to the soothing effect of holding the Core meditation device (which uses vibration and biofeedback). Apollo takes that concept further: it's worn continuously if desired, and its vibrations are precisely engineered and backed by some emerging research. Unlike traditional meditation aids, Apollo doesn't require you to stop and engage with it – you simply feel it in the background. This makes it attractive to those who want stress relief on the go, but it also raises healthy scepticism. Compared to doing breathing exercises or using an EEG headband, Apollo is completely passive; the user's role is just to notice the calming effect. This can complement a mindfulness routine (for instance, wearing Apollo during a guided meditation) or help those who struggle with anxiety to more easily get into a calm headspace.

23.5 Sensate 2 – Sound & Vagus Nerve Relaxation Pebble

Name: Sensate 2

Function: A pebble-like device that rests on your chest and uses vibration paired with sound to stimulate the vagus nerve and quickly induce calm. Sensate's approach is unique: you lie down, place the pebble on your sternum, put on headphones, and play one of the Sensate app's soundscapes. The device emits synchronized vibrations that resonate through your chest, directly stimulating the vagus nerve (a key nerve in the parasympathetic "rest and digest" system). The combination of the gentle humming vibrations and the ambient audio is intended to create a deep relaxation response – essentially an effortless meditation. The slogan "no-sweat serenity" has been used to describe Sensate's effect. Each session lasts about 10 to 30 minutes, and the system does not require any conscious effort aside from focusing on the sensations. Sensate doesn't record data or directly quantify your state (there's no HRV readout, for example). It's purely a relaxation aid.

Release Date: Sensate 2 launched around 2022 as an update to the original 2020 Sensate. It became more widely reviewed in 2023 as interest in vagus nerve stimulation grew.

Official Product Page: getsensate.com

Comparison: Sensate brings to mind some of the biofeedback relaxation techniques discussed earlier in the book, but it automates them. For instance, we learned about breathing exercises to stimulate the vagus nerve and trigger relaxation. Sensate achieves a similar outcome without the user having to breathe in any particular way – the device's vibration directly encourages the body's relaxation response. Sensate removes the "work" of pacing your breath and instead provides an external rhythm that calms you. One reviewer noted that the vibration and music are "surprisingly soothing" and give the anxious mind something to focus on, especially for those who struggle to meditate on their own. In tone, Sensate aligns with mindfulness ideals: it encourages you to lie quietly, be present with bodily sensations, and let go. But it's also very modern in that it leverages technology (sound and vibration) to facilitate an ancient goal (activating the body's natural relaxation). For readers familiar with meditation benchmates like calming music or weighted blankets, Sensate might be seen as a high-tech cousin of those, enhancing a restorative practice. It stands apart from the EEG and smart rings by not measuring progress – instead, it's about creating an immediate feeling of calm that can make subsequent meditation or sleep much easier.

23.6 Flow Neuroscience Headset – tDCS for Mood and Mental Wellness

Name: Flow Neuroscience Headset

Function: A wearable tDCS (transcranial direct current stimulation) device that delivers a gentle electric current to specific areas of the scalp to improve mood, attention, and mental well-being. The Flow headset is designed like a simple headband with electrode pads that sit on the forehead and above the ears. It sends a low-level current (2 milliamps) to the left frontal region of the brain, which research has linked to alleviating depression symptoms and enhancing neural activity in that area. Accompanying the device is a therapy app with guidance on mood, lifestyle (including meditation, exercise, and sleep tips). Users undergo 30-minute stimulation sessions, typically several times a week for a few weeks, as a course of treatment or brain training. By gently modulating brain activity, Flow aims to make it easier for individuals to achieve a balanced, non-depressed state, which can indirectly support engagement in mindfulness practices (when one's underlying anxiety or depression is reduced).

Release Date: Initially released in Europe in 2019 as a CE-certified at-home depression treatment. It entered broader public awareness by 2023–2024 as clinical trials validated its effects and it became available in more markets (UK and EU pharmacies).

Official Product Page: flowneuroscience.com

Comparison: In earlier chapters we covered neurostimulation devices based on technologies such as tDCS. The Flow headset is part of this same family of devices that actively stimulate the brain, but it's the first one squarely targeted at mental health and available direct-to-consumer in recent years. Flow is positioned as a user-friendly wellness gadget – you can self-administer tDCS at home with minimal supervision. Flow has a modern design and a focused purpose (treating depression and improving mood). It also integrates content: the app encourages you to build healthy habits like meditation, aligning well with the mindfulness theme (the company even cites mindfulness meditation as one pillar of their holistic approach).

23.7 Gadgets from Big Tech

Big tech has now fully entered the mindful gadget territory. Samsung launched the Galaxy Ring in July 2024, a dedicated smart ring for health and wellness tracking that monitors sleep, heart rate, and stress levels. Apple continues to expand its Health app and Apple Watch capabilities, adding mental wellness features and mood tracking from watchOS 10 (2023) onwards. The momentum in 2023–2025 is clear: mindfulness tech is becoming more wearable, more continuous, and more scientifically sophisticated. From finger rings to headbands and vibrating touch devices, the ecosystem of tools to support meditation and self-awareness is richer than ever. As always, the true value of these gadgets comes from how we use them – as aids to tune into ourselves, not as distractions. Used wisely, they can act as gentle guides and friends on our mindfulness journey, making it a little easier to cultivate calm and clarity in a busy world.

23.8 Mendi Headband – fNIRS Brain Training for Focus

The Mendi headband (https://www.mendi.io/) is a noteworthy alternative to EEG-based devices such as Muse and Neurosky. Rather than measuring electrical brain signals, Mendi uses functional near-infrared spectroscopy (fNIRS) – the same technology later combined with EEG in the Muse S Athena. fNIRS works by shining near-infrared light through the scalp to detect changes in blood flow and oxygen levels in the prefrontal cortex, which is the

brain region responsible for executive functions such as focus, decision-making, and emotional regulation.

The Mendi system works as follows: the headband is worn on the forehead and connects to a smartphone app via Bluetooth. As the user meditates or does a brain-training exercise, the app visualises their prefrontal cortex activity in real time through a simple gamified interface – a ball rises or falls on the screen based on the user's level of focused brain activity. The goal is to keep the ball rising, which indicates stronger activation of the prefrontal cortex.

Mendi has been used in research at institutions such as Stanford and Princeton University. According to aggregated user data, 84% of users reported better focus within three weeks of regular use. The device is especially suited to those who want to build concentration and emotional regulation, rather than track meditation specifically. It is priced more affordably than many EEG devices and has a 60-day money-back guarantee. For those in India, import duties may apply and should be factored into the total cost. As a meditation companion, Mendi is best used alongside sitting practice – the neurofeedback helps train the same mental muscle that mindfulness exercises, namely the ability to sustain attention and return to focus when the mind wanders.

23.9 Pulsetto – Wearable Vagus Nerve Stimulator

Pulsetto (https://pulsetto.tech/) is a wearable device worn around the neck that uses transcutaneous vagus nerve stimulation (tVNS) to induce relaxation and reduce stress. It is among the most accessible consumer-grade vagus nerve stimulation devices, positioned as a complement to existing meditation practices. The vagus nerve is the longest cranial nerve in the body and plays a crucial role in regulating mood, stress, digestion, heart rate, and sleep. By gently stimulating it, Pulsetto helps shift the nervous system from a sympathetic (fight-or-flight) state into a parasympathetic (rest-and-digest) state.

To use Pulsetto, the user applies a small amount of conductive gel to the electrodes and places the device on the neck. Sessions last between 4 and 10 minutes. Most users report a gentle tingling sensation and a noticeable shift toward calm within minutes. The accompanying app offers programs for stress, anxiety, burnout, sleep, and focus, along with guided meditations and breathing exercises. It can be used as a quick wind-down tool before a meditation session – the stimulation helps quieten the nervous system so that sitting in stillness becomes more natural. The device is priced around $200–$299 depending on the model, and is available internationally including via Amazon. While the clinical evidence base is still growing, a number of pilot studies have reported improvements in cortisol levels, sleep, and stress markers.

23.10 AI-Powered Meditation Apps: The Next Wave

A significant new trend emerging from 2023 onwards is the use of artificial intelligence to personalise meditation guidance. While apps such as Headspace, Calm, and Insight Timer introduced AI-based features to customise session recommendations based on user history and mood, a newer generation of apps goes further by dynamically generating meditation content in real time.

Notable examples include the following. Vital AI (https://joinvital.ai/) allows the user to type in a single word or sentence describing what they want to focus on and instantly generates a personalised spoken audio meditation session, complete with background music and a choice of voice. It supports techniques such as mindfulness, body scan, loving kindness, visualisation, and affirmations. Eiren AI (eiren.ai) takes a similar approach, tailoring sessions to the user's emotional input in real time and providing 5-, 10-, or 15-minute sessions in a voice of the user's choosing. Bliss Brain and Meditia are further examples of apps that combine large language model technology with guided meditation to deliver unique, individualised sessions on demand. Headspace has introduced an AI companion called "Ebb" that customises sessions, tracks stress patterns, and provides meditation analytics. Insight Timer, as of 2025, offers AI-powered tools to filter its library of over 260,000 free meditations by stress level, focus need, or time availability. Meanwhile, NeuroFit (neurofit.app) focuses on movement-based stress release, using AI to analyse biometric data from wearables and user input to recommend daily somatic exercises for nervous system regulation.

The global meditation devices and apps market is projected to grow from approximately $2.5 billion in 2023 to $7.5 billion by 2032, driven in part by AI-powered personalisation. AI meditation tools are particularly useful for practitioners who struggle with consistency – the ability to receive a meditation tailored to one's exact mood and available time lowers the barrier significantly. As with any technology, it is wise to use these tools intentionally and not become overly reliant on external input. However, as a gateway into regular practice, AI-generated meditation is a genuinely promising development. The ancient aspiration of having a personal meditation teacher whispering guidance into the ear of the practitioner has, in a sense, become technically possible at scale.

Chapter 24: LLMs, AI Agents, and Meditation Personas: A New Frontier

The AI-powered meditation apps described in the previous section represent one part of a much larger shift underway in the field of artificial intelligence. Beyond apps that generate guided audio sessions on demand, a new category of tool has emerged: large language models (LLMs) and AI agents that can hold open-ended conversations about meditation, act as practice companions, and even adopt dedicated meditation personas. This section explores how these technologies work, what they offer to the meditator, and where the genuine tensions lie.

24.1 What are LLMs and AI Agents?

A large language model (LLM) is an AI system trained on vast quantities of text that can generate fluent, contextually appropriate language in response to almost any input. Well-known examples include ChatGPT (by OpenAI), Claude (by Anthropic), and Gemini (by Google). These are not merely question-and-answer systems. They can hold extended conversations, explain complex topics in plain language, adapt their tone to the user's needs, and even take on specific roles or personas when instructed to do so.

An AI agent is a step further: it is an LLM that can take actions, remember information across sessions, search the web, call external tools, and pursue multi-step goals autonomously. While most consumer-facing LLM interfaces today are conversational, the agent layer adds the ability to monitor habits, schedule reminders, review journal entries over time, and even coordinate with other apps such as a smart home system or calendar. For meditation, this distinction is significant: a conversational LLM is like a knowledgeable companion you can ask anything, whereas an AI agent is more like an active coach that takes initiative on your behalf.

24.2 What LLMs Can Offer the Meditator

A general-purpose LLM such as Claude or ChatGPT, even without any special meditation app, can already serve as a surprisingly capable meditation companion. Some of the practical uses include the following.

First, on-demand guided session generation: a practitioner can describe their current state (anxious, tired, scattered, grieving) and ask the LLM to generate a personalised guided meditation tailored to exactly that moment. The model can incorporate specific traditions, imagery, duration, and tone on request. This is far more flexible than any pre-recorded audio library.

Second, tradition-aware instruction: an LLM trained on a wide corpus can explain the philosophy behind a technique, clarify the differences between Theravada, Zen, Vajrayana, Vedantic, and secular mindfulness approaches, and answer the practitioner's "why" questions with patience and depth. This kind of contextual dialogue is something a simple timer app cannot provide, and even many human teachers may lack the breadth to address across traditions.

Third, practice journal reflection: a practitioner can share notes about their meditation sessions and ask the LLM to identify patterns, note progress over time, or suggest adjustments. This mirrors what a skilled teacher does during a regular check-in, a form of support that most practitioners lack access to between retreat or class settings.

Fourth, adaptive real-time coaching: with voice-enabled interfaces, an LLM could listen as a practitioner describes what is arising during or after a session, and respond with gentle redirection, normalisation, or encouragement. This is still an emerging area, but the direction is clear.

24.3 AI Meditation Personas: The Contemplative Companion

One of the more unusual possibilities that LLMs open up is the creation of AI personas tailored specifically to contemplative purposes. A developer or even a non-technical user can instruct an LLM to adopt the character of a calm, unhurried presence: a Zen teacher, a forest monk, a Vedantic sage, or simply a wise and patient friend who never rushes. The persona shapes not just the content of the responses but their tone, pacing, and even the quality of silence implied in the interaction.

This matters because meditation practice is not purely informational. The relational container in which guidance is offered has its own effect. Being met by a presence that is calm, non-judgmental, and unhurried creates conditions that support settling of the mind. Even if the "presence" is synthetic, research in human-computer interaction suggests that the felt quality of the interaction still influences the user's psychological state. A warmly framed response from a contemplative AI persona can have a measurably different effect from the same information delivered in a clinical tone.

India's contemplative traditions are especially rich territory for this kind of persona work. An AI designed around the voice and teachings of the Advaita tradition, for example, could guide users through self-inquiry in the manner of Ramana Maharshi's dialogues. A persona grounded in Vipassana tradition could walk practitioners through the stages of insight described in the Pali Canon. These are not replacements for authentic lineage transmission, but they can serve as valuable orientation for beginners and a reflective surface for more experienced practitioners.

24.4 The Indian Context: Access and Tradition

For Indian readers, the intersection of LLMs and contemplative practice has particular relevance. India is both a cradle of the world's most sophisticated meditation traditions and home to one of the largest and fastest-growing populations of smartphone users. Many practitioners, especially in smaller cities and rural areas, have no easy access to qualified meditation teachers. An LLM-powered companion available in Hindi, Tamil, Bengali, or other regional languages, familiar with both classical Indian spiritual texts and modern mindfulness research, could serve a democratising function similar to what mobile apps have already begun to do, but with far greater depth and responsiveness.

India's wellness industry is also large and growing rapidly. LLM-based meditation companions represent a natural extension of the existing app ecosystem described in Chapter 10, but with the added dimension of conversation, memory, and personalisation. Indian startups and global platforms alike are beginning to explore this space, and it is likely to be a significant area of product development over the next several years.

24.5 Genuine Tensions Worth Considering

As with all the technologies described in this book, it would be premature to offer uncritical enthusiasm. Several concerns deserve honest attention.

The first is authenticity. Meditation traditions, especially those grounded in lineage and direct transmission from teacher to student, place great emphasis on the living quality of instruction. An AI persona can mimic the form of such a relationship with considerable skill, but whether anything essential is lost in that mimicry is a question that deserves serious contemplation. Practitioners who feel drawn to traditional paths should be encouraged to seek out authentic teachers and communities, and to use AI tools as a supplement rather than a substitute.

The second is dependency. An engaging and responsive AI companion could paradoxically deepen a practitioner's reliance on external input rather than cultivating the self-sufficiency and inward stability that most traditions ultimately aim for. The goal of meditation, in many frameworks, is to need less and less — including, eventually, less instruction and fewer props. An AI meditation companion should ideally point the practitioner toward their own experience rather than becoming a habit in itself.

The third is the overstimulation of the conceptual mind. LLMs work through language and ideas, which are precisely the faculties that deeper meditation practice aims to settle and, in some traditions, dissolve. A practitioner who spends twenty minutes discussing their meditation session with an AI may inadvertently reinforce the very conceptual activity they are trying to quieten. Used with awareness, an LLM can be a useful pre- or post-session tool. Used unconsciously, it may work against the practice.

The fourth, and perhaps the most philosophically interesting, is what might be called the stillness problem. The best meditation instruction often lies in knowing when to say nothing. Silence, space, and the absence of direction can be as powerful as any technique. Current LLMs are trained to respond, to fill the conversational space with helpfulness. Designing an AI that is genuinely comfortable with not responding, that can sit with the practitioner in virtual silence, is a challenge that no product has yet fully solved.

24.6 Looking Ahead

The most promising near-term development is probably not the replacement of human teachers by AI personas, but the extension of access. Millions of people in India and around the world who are genuinely interested in meditation have no teacher, no sangha, no community of practice. For them, a thoughtful, knowledgeable, and warmly patient AI companion could serve as a genuine gateway into regular practice, and a bridge toward the human connections that ultimately sustain it.

As with wearable gadgets, apps, and all the other technologies described in this book, the key principle remains the same: no tool can substitute for the practitioner's own intention, attention, and willingness to turn inward. Used wisely, LLMs and AI agents can be intelligent, flexible, and even inspiring companions on that journey. Used unconsciously, they are simply another screen. The choice, as always, lies with the meditator.

Chapter 25: Conclusion

In this book, we explored a wide variety of gadgets, wearables, apps, and smart tools that support meditation and mindfulness practice. From EEG headbands and HRV-based smart rings to meditation lamps, float tanks, and AI-guided companions, we've seen how modern technology can be harnessed to enhance well-being and deepen meditative awareness. The tools and gadgets described in this book may be more useful to beginners, to those involved in sedentary technology or software work or to those who simply want a break from daily stress.

Still, some would say that nothing can substitute a good teacher and a good meditation sitting, for which such apps are not of much use. In the end both can complement each other: a regular meditation practice or extended meditation retreat can be complemented by such apps and wearables for daily use.

Meditation, at its core, is a natural and timeless human practice. It requires no tools—only presence. However, in today's fast-paced, distraction-filled world, technology can offer gentle nudges and external supports to help us cultivate consistency and depth in our practice. When used mindfully, tech can become an ally on the inner journey.

We began with foundational tools like fitness trackers and HRV monitors, which offer objective biofeedback on how our bodies respond to stillness. We then looked at more advanced gadgets like EEG devices (Muse, Neurosky) and immersive experiences like VR headsets and float tanks. These tools offer novel and sometimes profound ways to access states of calm, relaxation, and focus.

We also examined newer trends, such as AI-guided meditations, smart home integration, and digital minimalism. These additions reflect the evolving nature of the modern meditator's toolkit, showing that mindfulness can be brought into our daily lives through smart routines, scheduled reminders, and even ambient lighting and soundscapes.

At the same time, we explored the wisdom of traditional paths—such as the Buddhist Jhanas, Yogic dhyana, and the Dzogchen and Zen views—which remind us that meditation is not about chasing scores or gamifying silence. Rather, it's about developing a stable, clear, and compassionate presence. Metrics can guide us, but they are not the goal.

Ultimately, mindfulness is not in the device—it's in how we use it. A smart ring or app can bring awareness to breath or posture, but only our intention and attention can truly transform our state of mind.

As you continue your exploration, we invite you to find a balance that works for you: between tradition and technology, stillness and signals, silence and sound. Let your tools serve your awareness, not distract from it.

We hope this book has offered you useful insights and practical suggestions for building your own mindful routine with the help of modern gadgets. May your journey be joyful, grounded, and filled with presence.

About the authors

Joy Bose is a data scientist and software engineer by profession. He lives and works in Bangalore, India. He has practiced meditation in multiple traditions including mindfulness meditation and Vajrayana, and is keenly interested in applications of technology in the field of meditation.

Siva Prasad Bose is an author of introductory guidebooks on aspects of Indian laws. He is currently retired after many years of service as an electrical engineer in Uttar Pradesh Power Corporation Limited. He received his engineering degree from Jadavpur University, Kolkata and has a law degree from Meerut University, Meerut and a BSc from MMH College, Ghaziabad. His interests lie in the fields of family law, civil law, law of contracts, and areas of law related to power electricity related issues. He lives in Delhi.

Other Books by Siva Prasad Bose

Introduction to Wills and Probate

Senior Citizens Abuse in India

Introduction to Negotiable Instruments

Introduction to Marriage Laws in India

Neighbor Problems in India and what to do about them

Delays in Court Cases in India

Self-Publish Books and E-Books in India

Introduction to Patents and Patent Law in India

Introduction to Property Law in India

About the Author

Joy Bose is a data scientist and software engineer by profession. He lives and works in Bangalore, India. He has practiced meditation in multiple traditions including mindfulness meditation and Vajrayana, and is keenly interested in applications of technology in the field of meditation.

www.ingramcontent.com/pod-product-compliance
Lightning Source LLC
Chambersburg PA
CBHW031332160726
47993CB00002B/632